The New York Times

RELAX AND UNWIND CROSSWORDS

6/28

The New York Times

RELAX AND UNWIND CROSSWORDS
75 Easy Puzzles

Edited by Will Shortz

ST. MARTIN'S GRIFFIN   NEW YORK

ACROSS

1 Rand McNally publication
6 Where a fetus develops
10 What says "Miss America" on Miss America
14 "Grand" instrument
15 Samoan capital
16 Duo + one
17 Cent
18 Casual pants
20 Ocean bottoms
22 Depart
23 Fishing line holder
24 Names like Billy the Kid
26 Vehicle with a compactor
30 Ingredient in a McDonald's Quarter Pounder
31 Recreational walk
32 Traffic problem
35 Unsuave sort
36 Unrefined oil
38 Conceal
39 Items checked by T.S.A. agents
40 Rugmaking apparatus
41 Target, as with a gun
42 Where one might witness a hit and run?
45 Opposite of rejects
48 Winnie-the-___
49 Find, as a missing person
50 Atomic bomb unit
53 Fishing gear holder
56 Stop, as a stream
58 "What ___ be done?"
59 Made a rug, e.g.
60 Pig sounds
61 Spot for a goatee

62 Spots for glasses
63 Skedaddles . . . or what 18-, 26-, 42- and 53-Across all have

DOWN

1 Online store offering
2 Knots
3 Roadway division
4 University of Michigan's home
5 Small source of protein
6 Walk like a duck
7 Magnum ___
8 Fraction of an hr.
9 Valise
10 What a meteor looks like in the sky
11 Zones
12 One working out the lumps?
13 Garden watering aids
19 Wonderland girl
21 Neural activity measure, for short
24 Desertlike
25 Book between Mark and John
26 Asian desert
27 "And giving ___, up the chimney he rose"
28 Spanish waterways
29 Hitchhiker's digit
32 Iwo ___
33 Eve's mate
34 Ration (out)
36 Price
37 Masses of fish eggs
38 Leave lickety-split
40 Place to pin a tiny flag
41 Numerous

42 Summon
43 Peaks
44 Item resting on andirons
45 Room just under a roof
46 Stock market disaster
47 Desert plants
50 Transport
51 Prefix with directional
52 Zap
54 Ram's mate
55 The "B" of B.S.A.
57 Letter add-ons, for short

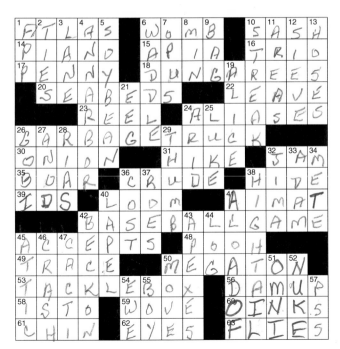

by Dave Sarpola

2

ACROSS

1 Shooter through whitewater rapids
5 Cold war inits.
9 Neatnik's opposite
13 Visitor for the holidays, maybe
15 Soothing plant
16 ___ Krishna
17 New Zealand native
18 Minor collision reminder
19 Wall Street Journal ___
20 On the front
23 Habitual drunk
25 Ship unit or shipping unit
26 Plow driver's handful
27 On the back
32 Buenos ___
33 Greedy person's demand
34 ___ of Sharon
35 Overexcited
37 Immediately, on a memo
41 Converge
42 Common blockage locale
43 On both sides
47 Symbol on a "This way" sign
49 "I kiss'd thee ___ I kill'd thee": Othello
50 Kind of scan
51 20-, 27- and 43-Across locale, in slang
56 Boneheaded
57 Gang woman
58 Macaroni, e.g.
61 And others: Abbr.
62 The thought that counts?
63 Compassion
64 Turn down
65 Metalworker's tool
66 Horse-pulled cart

DOWN

1 Air balls miss it
2 Santa ___
3 People in 1-Acrosses, e.g.
4 Alpine lake
5 Rhythmic
6 Something of interest to Miss Marple
7 "And" or "or": Abbr.
8 Antifur org.
9 Drinks with straws
10 CBS series for 17 seasons
11 The Hunter
12 Jack's purchase in a children's story
14 C, D and EEE
21 Le ___ Soleil
22 Mötley ___
23 White dwarf, e.g.

24 The Allegheny and Monongahela join to form it
28 Like Willie Winkie
29 Evacuate
30 Furrow maker
31 Hockey defender Bobby
35 Egg layer
36 For the present
37 Feel unwell
38 Establishment that might sell 9-Down and 53-Downs
39 Glow
40 [Hey, buddy!]
41 Whimper
42 Miss Marple, e.g.
43 Winner of 1948
44 Not stable
45 Iguana feature
46 Sphere
47 Supplementary

48 A FedEx driver may have one
52 Arab ruler
53 Drink with a straw
54 Naughty Goose and Moose Drool
55 Readied to play
59 Cy Young's was 2.63, in brief
60 Pig's home

by John Guzzetta

ACROSS

1 1970 #1 hit with the lyric "Easy as . . ."
4 Last option, often
9 Equally poor
14 Miracle-___
15 Soap genre
16 Macbeth or Macduff
17 Surgically replaceable body parts
19 With 49-Across, jumble
20 Sop up
21 Many a corporate plane
23 On videotape, say
24 Supposed skill of some hotline operators
27 The sun, in Spain
28 Some INTs result in them
29 When mammoths roamed
31 Sedona automaker
33 On-the-spot appraisal
36 "___ directed"
39 Sun-kissed
40 Tea-growing Indian state
41 Classic mountain bikes
44 H.R.H. part
45 Alternative to texts
46 Manhattan's crosstown arteries: Abbr.
49 See 19-Across
52 Cards, on scoreboards
53 Green "pet"
54 Bar musicians may put them out
56 Total nonsense
58 "___ the loneliest number"
59 Serving with syrup
62 Lee and Laurel
63 As such

64 Merry Prankster Kesey
65 The hotheaded Corleone
66 Protected from rainouts, say
67 Sellout sign

DOWN

1 Terror-struck
2 Greased the palm of
3 Thickets
4 Foot problem
5 Manhattan film festival locale
6 ___ Solo (Ford role)
7 Defib operator
8 Sing like Tom Waits
9 Playwright Fugard
10 Hits the "Add to Cart" button and then continues, say
11 Elicitors of groans

12 Actress Jolie
13 Bug repellent
18 Stewart in the "Wordplay" documentary
22 Action hero's underwater breathing aid
25 Body part that may be deviated
26 Nightwear . . . or a hidden feature of 17-, 21-, 33-, 41-, 54- and 59-Across?
29 Clouseau, e.g.: Abbr.
30 Defensive excavation
32 PIN requester
33 "Casablanca" pianist
34 Needle-nosed swimmers
35 Ed.'s workload
36 Work the aisles, informally

37 Put on, as pants
38 Like some Turks and Georgians
42 Give the raspberry
43 Basic orbital path
46 Tases, say
47 Bygone Wall Street device
48 Refuses
50 Spirit of Islamic myth
51 Like a blowhard
53 "The Bourne Supremacy" org.
54 Eject from the game
55 Dirty Harry's org.
57 Handled the music at a rave
60 DiCaprio, to pals
61 Escort's offering

by Pete Muller

4

ACROSS

1 Woman in a choir
5 Scribbled, say
10 One piece of a three-piece suit
14 Lav
15 "Horrible" comic strip character
16 Sound in a long hallway
17 Golden ___ (senior)
18 Tennis champ Agassi
19 Provoke
20 Neckwear for princes?
22 Jiggly dessert
23 Calendar pgs.
24 Neckwear for a full baseball team?
26 Alternative to "shape up"
30 Vote for
31 The "p" in r.p.m.
32 Neckwear just right for the occasion?
38 Have a life
41 U.K. honour
42 Posturepedic maker
43 Neckwear for informal occasions?
46 ___ rummy
47 Top of a woman's swimsuit
48 City that a song asks "Do you know the way to . . . ?"
51 Neckwear for boyfriends?
56 "O Sole ___"
57 States with confidence
58 Neckwear in a work of fiction?
63 Rosemary, for one
64 Blew it
65 Doughnut shapes, mathematically
66 Song in a libretto
67 Andrea ___ (ship in 1956 headlines)
68 Furry ally of Luke Skywalker
69 Major Calif.-to-Fla. route
70 With cunning
71 100-yard race, e.g.

DOWN

1 Cracked a little
2 Target's target, e.g.
3 He and she
4 Entrance to a freeway
5 "Anything going on?"
6 Indian princess
7 Nash who loved to rhyme
8 Ankle bones
9 Byron's "before"
10 Do nothing
11 Food-poisoning bacteria
12 Oil-producing rock
13 Fusses
21 Lav
22 Derisive shouts
25 Bill ___, the Science Guy
26 Design detail, for short
27 Six: Prefix
28 Pupil surrounder
29 Harness race gait
33 Japanese sash
34 What "Peter Piper picked a peck of pickled peppers" has a lot of
35 Villain who says "O, beware, my lord, of jealousy"
36 Yale students, informally
37 "Auld Lang ___"
39 Like bedroom communities
40 Bite-size pies, maybe
44 China's Chou En-___
45 Expeditious type of delivery
49 Goose egg
50 Scribbled (down)
51 Faith founded in 19th-century Persia
52 Turn inside out
53 Eagle's nest
54 Become a member: Var.
55 "My bad"
59 Part of a bridal ensemble
60 Des Moines's state
61 Arrow shooter of Greek myth
62 Worshiper in a temple
64 Magazine staffers, for short

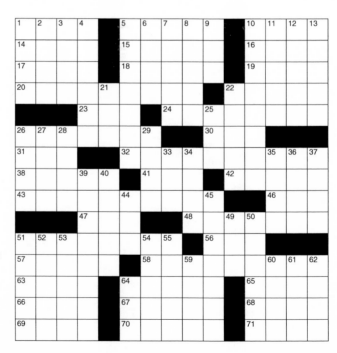

by Tom Pepper

ACROSS

1 Verdi duet "Madre, non ___?"
6 Gucci rival
11 Wheelwright's tool
14 Cousins of foils
15 Strange
16 Narrow inlet
17 Cows, pigs and chickens
19 Equivalent of about seven cases of beer
20 Watery
21 Deep-toned instrument
23 Sister
24 Location of Mount McKinley
29 Mural surface
31 ___ the Lip (major-league nickname)
32 Buddy of "The Beverly Hillbillies"
33 UPS delivery: Abbr.
35 See 26-Down
37 Masculine side
38 One can be found in each of the answers to 17-, 24-, 54- and 63-Across
43 Gen. Robt. ___
44 Otto's vehicle on "The Simpsons"
45 Italian article
46 Frighten
48 Do a voice-over for
50 Out of touch with reality
54 A.M. or F.M. news dispatch
57 Baseball scoreboard letters
58 Cream-toned
59 Certain sedatives
61 Gun, as an engine
63 Sprain, say
66 Alcindor : Abdul-Jabbar :: Clay : ___
67 Direct (to)
68 French square

69 Inits. on a bottle of Parisienne
70 Tin Pan Alley output
71 Aikman and Donahue

DOWN

1 Render harmless, as a snake
2 Impossible to see through
3 "Seinfeld" episodes, now
4 Idea that may spread via the Internet
5 Japanese-born P.G.A. star
6 Former Saudi king
7 Blight victim
8 Actress Vardalos
9 The Mississippi has a big one
10 Cover, in a way

11 Bill Clinton, by birth
12 Go out, as a fire
13 Turn back sharply
18 Void, in Versailles
22 Where one might get one's first pair of overalls
25 Lampoons
26 Bryant of the 35-Across
27 There's one for curly hair
28 56-Down grad: Abbr.
30 Ball-like
34 Hunk
36 Tempe sch.
38 Be frightened
39 Teatro ___ Scala
40 Manta
41 Like the athletes in the ancient Olympics

42 You might not think to use it
47 Quagmire
49 Pro wrestling fans, frequently
51 Conductor Toscanini
52 Sundae topper
53 "You're right, absolutely"
55 Total
56 Upstate N.Y. sch.
60 Like a door that doesn't afford complete privacy
61 Manta, e.g.
62 Loop transports
64 "Brainiac" author Jennings
65 Calf's place

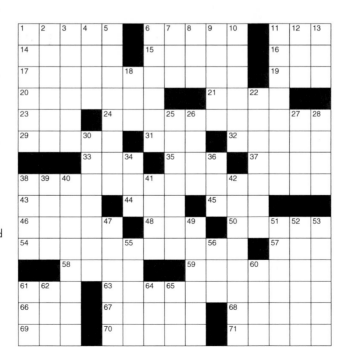

by Bill Thompson

6

ACROSS

1 Mlles., across the border
6 Big bird
9 Clear up, in a way
14 Verb in "The Raven"
15 PC connection
16 Word on a lawn sign
17 Free from bondage
19 Send sky-high
20 Gore and Green
21 Cinema chain
22 Something that's good to break
23 Handed down, as lore
25 Stops procrastinating
27 Frivolous gal of song
30 Aldous Huxley's school
31 Collections of like objects
33 "Silas Marner" girl
36 Lapsed, as a subscription
37 Trademark of 1899 that's no longer protected
40 Stirs up
41 Hit the gas
42 Atlas feature
43 Expose to UV waves, say
45 Connections to the WWW
49 S.S.S. part: Abbr.
50 Devotees: Suffix
51 Exactly right
53 Quizzical utterances
55 See 1-Down
57 Coach Parseghian
58 Hoops Hall-of-Famer Thomas
60 Italian P.M. nicknamed Divo Giulio
62 Uniform decoration

63 Excessive detail, in a text
64 Mad magazine's "___ Gang of Idiots"
65 Smart-alecky
66 Yet, in verse
67 Hamilton vs. Burr and others

DOWN

1 With 55-Across, what the circled letters, reading clockwise, form
2 Brook
3 Throw in the direction of
4 Greek capital, to airlines
5 Intend to definitely
6 Sommer of film
7 Viruses, worms, etc.
8 Intl. peace and human rights grp.
9 Distant regions of the universe
10 First name in scat
11 Is intrepid
12 Thanksgiving mo., in Canada
13 Co. that merged into Verizon
18 Salted fish
24 Five Nations tribe
26 Spins, rolls or draws
28 Malaria symptom
29 Normandy vessels of '44
31 Martini base, maybe
32 Ab ___ (from the beginning)
34 In a Victorian manner
35 Larklike songbird
37 Floor model caveat

38 Nimble for one's age
39 August meteor shower
40 Suffix with serpent
42 "My treat"
44 Fill with gas
46 Center of many a plaza
47 Way in
48 Slimy pests
51 Orch. section
52 Pretentious sort
54 Lukas of "Witness"
56 Asgard ruler
58 Some AOL transmissions
59 Chantey subject
61 The Cowboys of the N.C.A.A.

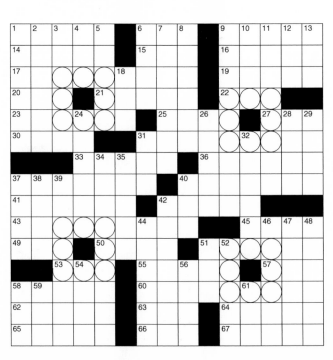

by Peter Koetters

ACROSS

1 Acad. or univ.
4 Starring role
8 Bieber with the 2010 hit "Baby"
14 Lyricist Gershwin
15 Olympic event with electrified equipment
16 Presume
17 Lean-___ (temporary shelters)
18 Squeezing tool
19 Not checked for speed
20 It's measured by polls
23 Height: Prefix
24 Home of the San Diego Padres
27 Tank engine of children's fiction
30 "Never mind"
31 Some jeans
33 Hurt
35 Be fond of
38 Dog's bark
39 Conqueror of the Incas
44 Pro's opposite
45 Mexican snack
46 Some cameras, for short
47 Frankie Valli's "___ Take My Eyes Off You"
49 Alphabetically first state: Abbr.
51 Seaport SE of Roma
55 Traveler to Cathay
59 Supply-and-demand subj.
60 Sting operative . . . or a hint to 20-, 24-, 39- and 55-Across
63 Make obsolete
66 Portent
67 Actress Thurman
68 Flies
69 Festooned with bathroom tissue, informally
70 Campus in Troy, N.Y.
71 Leather worker
72 Sailors
73 ___ Andreas fault

DOWN

1 Decide against making any changes
2 Catcher's stance
3 Company that makes Scrabble
4 Jeans maker Strauss
5 Awesome, in slang
6 Fable writer
7 Get worse, as losses
8 Month after mayo
9 Slangy request for a high-five
10 Kind of cord or column
11 Male turkey
12 Suffix with expert
13 Beatty of "Charlie Wilson's War"
16 Frito-Lay product once sold in a 100% compostable bag
21 The salesman in "Death of a Salesman"
22 Author Calvino
25 Rump
26 Deborah of "The King and I"
28 Bank holding: Abbr.
29 Sunni rival
32 California's second-busiest airport, after LAX
34 Fugitives
36 Pottery oven
37 Poet Pound
39 Media monitoring grp.
40 Move aimlessly
41 26-Down's role in "The King and I"
42 1950s TV innovation
43 "___ our agreement . . ."
48 Whom "Dewey Defeats" in a classic Chicago Tribune headline
50 "Little Women" author
52 Takes place
53 See 58-Down
54 Hurting
56 Bill worth 100 smackers
57 More peculiar
58 With 53-Down, Willy Wonka employee
61 Swerve
62 Finales
63 Kellogg's Cracklin' ___ Bran
64 The Cavaliers of the A.C.C.
65 Its atomic symbol is Sn

by Joel Fagliano

8

ACROSS

1 Mediterranean and Baltic, in Monopoly: Abbr.
5 Org. suggested by the starts of 17-, 31-, 41- and 62-Across
9 Kind of point
14 Tora ___ (Afghan area)
15 Pop
16 One of the Dutch Antilles
17 Pricey accommodations on a ship
20 HI hi
21 Kaput
22 Fruit drink
23 One who knows his beans?
26 In a row
28 "I ___ what I said"
30 "+" thing
31 Ward worker
38 Like some highly-rated bonds
39 Grant-giving org.
40 Dog command
41 What disabled people are entitled to on a subway
48 Mich./Minn. separator
49 Sei + uno
50 Bell site
54 "Hmmm . . ."
58 "___ ba-a-ack!"
59 Hemingway's nickname
61 Words after hang or dash
62 Quick way to pay
66 Maker of Aleve
67 Western tribe
68 Prefix with European
69 Little helpers?
70 5-Across's business
71 Olympic female gymnast, typically

DOWN

1 '90s–'00s Britcom
2 "Ta-da!"
3 Overthrowing a base, e.g.
4 Menu item often accompanied by wasabi
5 Pac-12 school, for short
6 Roman sun god
7 Droids, e.g.
8 Obama girl
9 Group within a group
10 Man-mouse link
11 Like the rumba, originally
12 Tolerate
13 Like interstates
18 Shocks, in a way
19 Sphere or pyramid
24 Bit of body art, informally
25 Regarding
27 Beast with a beard
29 Low poker holdings
31 Jay-Z's genre
32 Musician's asset
33 Moo goo ___ pan
34 Hotel meeting room amenity
35 Hitter's stat
36 Statehouse worker: Abbr.
37 A snake may swallow one whole
42 Part of i.o.u.
43 Bodice-___ (old-fashioned romance novels)
44 Puerto Rico y La Española
45 Summer on the 55-Down
46 High level?
47 Do-it-yourself diagnostic tool
50 Biblical land on the Arabian Peninsula
51 ___-size (big)
52 Awards won by LeBron James and David Beckham
53 British racetrack site
55 Rhône feeder
56 Avoid
57 Rocker John
60 Court records
63 Like many seniors: Abbr.
64 ___ polloi
65 Wriggly fish

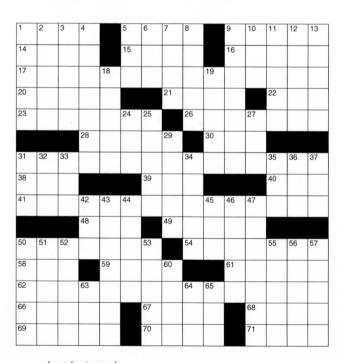

by Jules P. Markey

ACROSS

1 Cavalry weapon
6 "And there it is!"
10 Argue (with)
14 Spasm
15 Hollywood has some big ones
16 Summon
17 Actor Norris, after gaining weight?
19 Attendee of the fictional Lowood Institution for girls
20 ". . . __ quit!"
21 Symbols of speed
22 Flower part
23 1993 Peace Nobelist
25 Hankering
26 What a tosspot fantasizes the clouds would do?
30 Designed to pique interest, say
33 Toot
34 Collar
36 "Hurry!"
37 Some makeup . . . or a hint to 17-, 26-, 43- and 58-Across
39 Badlands feature
40 Unite
41 Whoosh!
42 A bit questionable
43 Thieves at an all-night dance bash?
47 Show some respect to a judge
48 All riled up
52 Emo emotion
54 Conceived
56 Sugar ending
57 Strike
58 Someone responding to a party R.S.V.P.?
60 __ Krabappel, Bart Simpson's teacher
61 Boxer's fare?
62 Kind of glasses
63 Dieter's amount
64 Paint swatch choice
65 Common door sign

DOWN

1 Longtime senator Thurmond
2 Now, in Nogales
3 Bobby Orr, notably
4 Impatient person's wait, seemingly
5 Conan O'Brien, e.g.
6 Mideast capital
7 Bad fit
8 Entries in two Oscar categories, slangily
9 "That's all I __"
10 Address
11 There used to be a lot more of these on corners
12 Indian tourist locale
13 Country dance
18 District of Colombia?
22 Knock off
24 Stalactite producer
25 Knocks off
27 Manhattan Project result, informally
28 Guitarist Paul
29 Shipboard punishment
30 Bar topic
31 PC operator
32 Items for baseball scouts and highway patrol officers
35 Triple Crown winner Citation or Gallant Fox
37 Reason for an R rating
38 Back of a public house, maybe
39 Get wrong
41 Spice
42 Where many Greeks are found
44 Outlooks
45 Part that may be pinched
46 Sufficiently, in poetry
49 Tribal figure
50 Rhône tributary
51 Put on again
52 Jump on the ice
53 Intersection point
54 Western accessory
55 N.F.L. broadcaster
58 __ in hand
59 Subj. of a Wall Street Journal story

by Ian Livengood

ACROSS

1 Indian tribe with a rain dance
5 Wood-shaping tool
8 Kind of tire
14 The answer to a preacher's prayers?
15 Org. with sniffing dogs
16 Old Soviet naval base site
17 Devour
19 Some online ads
20 "You cheated!"
21 Cooler contents
23 New York's Tappan ___ Bridge
24 Waste time playfully
28 Buffalo Bill
31 Teacher after a test, e.g.
32 "Honest" prez
33 File folder projection
35 Choice of a political party
39 Pay what's due
41 Eat, eat, eat
42 Porky's porcine sweetie
44 Tyrannosaurus ___
45 Right-to-bear-arms org.
46 Carter's successor
48 Chimney sweep coating
49 Hoard
54 Crude home
55 Uganda's ___ Amin
56 Attached ___ (legalese phrase)
60 Crops up
63 Pertain to
65 Like Jim Crow laws
66 "Don't you know who ___?"
67 Lima's land
68 Makes into law
69 Boffo show sign
70 Hankerings

DOWN

1 "The First Wives Club" actress Goldie
2 Melville opus
3 Ill-gotten wealth
4 Criminal renown
5 Deck out
6 Pasture moisture
7 More madcap
8 Muhammad Ali strategy
9 "Much ___ About Nothing"
10 Withdrawal's opposite: Abbr.
11 Japanese truck maker
12 "Quaking" tree
13 Erased a tattoo, say
18 God, in Italian
22 Blue shade
25 Spy grp. dissolved in 1991
26 Many a song at a dance club
27 Not a photocopy: Abbr.
28 Al who created Joe Btfsplk
29 Instrument with metal keys
30 Tin can blemish
33 One doing piano repair
34 Beekeepers
36 It's taboo
37 Continental coin
38 Coup d'___
40 Space race hero Gagarin
43 Superannuated
44 Genetic material
47 They may fall apart under cross-examination
48 Too sentimental
49 Not hoard
50 Imam's holy book
51 New York city with a name from antiquity
52 Company that originated Frisbees and Boogie Boards
53 ___ Lingus
57 Sporting sword
58 Ripped
59 Big burden
61 [not my mistake]
62 Superlative suffix
64 What a headphone goes over

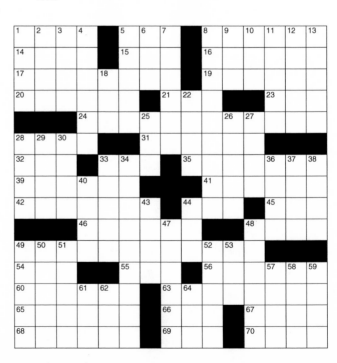

by Gareth Bain

ACROSS

1 Singer Lou
6 Latin 101 word
10 Mystery writer John Dickson ___
14 Bubbling over
15 ___ Ness
16 Double curve
17 Competition for 3-year-olds
18 Together, musically
19 "The Lion King" lioness
20 Breastbones
22 Resin in varnish
24 Prefix with -batics
25 Supplicate
26 City in Ukraine or Texas
29 Gourmand
30 Roy G. ___
31 Haughty response
33 Something that makes stops on the ocean?
37 Frozen drink brand
39 Mythical hunter
41 "The Time Machine" race
42 Medicinal plant
44 ___ throat
46 Rock genre
47 Pear variety
49 "The Hitler Diaries" and others
51 Subgroup
54 Gator's cousin
55 Strong spate
56 Like many eighth graders
60 White House policy honcho
61 Out
63 Grammy winner Ronstadt
64 Onetime Sony competitor
65 Staff member?
66 To have, to Henri
67 Veg out
68 Poetic adverb
69 O. Henry Award winner for "Livvie Is Back"

DOWN

1 Units of a dangerous dosage
2 Aid's partner
3 Sported
4 Some fall babies
5 Craft
6 1836 battle site
7 Certain '60s teens
8 Prefix with puncture
9 Venue where Toscanini conducted
10 Be green, in a way
11 Marble material
12 Archaeologist's find
13 Get through to
21 Heavens: Prefix
23 Where Billy Budd went in "Billy Budd"
25 Ulan ___, Mongolia
26 Some wraps
27 Backgammon needs
28 Like certain odds, paradoxically
29 Verdi aria
32 Director Welles
34 Quizmaster Trebek
35 A portion of
36 Madre's brothers
38 F flat equivalent
40 Jacket style
43 Spanish liqueur
45 Old welfare measure
48 Composer Strauss
50 Not retired
51 Kind of point
52 1944 battle site
53 Rush hour speed
54 More coquettish
56 It may be tempted
57 Carbon compound
58 Do some paperwork
59 ___ a soul
62 Trial

by Alex Vratsanos

ACROSS

1 Quick wit
7 Billy of "Titanic"
11 "Eternally nameless" Chinese principle
14 In harm's way
15 Ruler of Asgard
16 Tool with a curved head
17 64-Across ingredient
19 "From my cold, dead hands!" sloganeer
20 "Elephant Boy" boy
21 64-Across ingredient
23 Bireme or trireme tool
25 "On the other hand . . ."
26 Andean wool source
27 Eve who wrote "The Vagina Monologues"
30 Commotion
31 Capt. Jean-___ Picard
32 Relax
36 "___ Ben Adhem"
40 64-Across ingredient
43 "Wait! There's more . . ."
44 Relax
45 French seasoning
46 GPS display features: Abbr.
48 Strut one's stuff, say
50 Illinois senator who became president
53 Jacuzzi sigh
56 Muscle car in a 1964 song
57 64-Across ingredient
60 Some calls to smokeys
63 Cousin ___ of '60s TV
64 "Macbeth" recipe

66 Flock formation
67 Prefix with -logical
68 Banned book of 1955
69 PC key
70 "A Doll's House" wife
71 Playwright Bertolt

DOWN

1 Snacks on
2 Greek colonnade
3 Notable nose
4 Fraternity initiation, e.g.
5 Roughly: Suffix
6 Some referee calls, for short
7 "Fantabulous!"
8 Take up, as a cause
9 Zeros, in soccer
10 Wrap around
11 Tucker who sang "Delta Dawn"
12 Pertinent, in law

13 Conductor Seiji
18 It may be embarrassing if it's open
22 Rose Parade entry
24 Bassoon part in two pieces
27 Isle of exile
28 Lacking value
29 Singer of 1976's "You'll Never Find Another Love Like Mine"
30 Church recesses
33 The Great Lakes' ___ Locks
34 Suffix with ranch
35 Stalling-for-time syllables
37 Seat of a Catholic official
38 Draft-ready
39 Hard on the eyes

41 "Goodbye, ___ Jean . . ."
42 Grab onto
47 Australian city named after a naturalist
49 Hospital condition
50 Antipasto bit
51 What fishermen hope for
52 Member of an empire ruled by the Mexica
53 Cousin of a daisy
54 Name in kitchen foil
55 Villain's chuckle
58 Lover of Aeneas
59 Peter ___, general manager of the Met
61 Aleph follower
62 Police jacket letters
65 College women's grp.

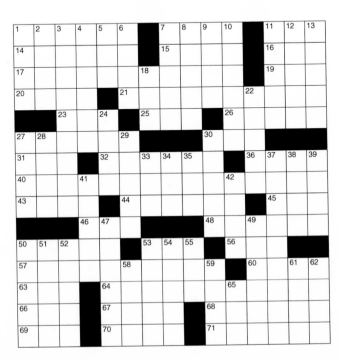

by Stu Ockman

ACROSS

1 Brad of "Moneyball"
5 Ibuprofen brand
10 Zoom up
14 5-Across target
15 U.S. 1's northern terminus
16 "Alas!"
17 Fishing line holder
18 Crime started with a match
19 Gas in commercial lights
20 Wynken's fishing buddies
23 French friend
25 Poem whose title might start "To a . . ."
26 Brings in, as money
27 Moe's slapstick pals
32 Sound portion of a broadcast
33 Ayn who wrote "Atlas Shrugged"
34 Bit of smoke
35 In the know
37 Concordes, e.g., for short
41 More than a quiz
42 Secret stash
43 Huey's fellow nephews
47 Dictation expert
49 Yvette's "yes"
50 "Lucy in the Sky With Diamonds" subject, supposedly
51 Snap's cereal mates
56 Make over completely
57 In base eight
58 Great Salt Lake site
61 "Well, did you ___?!"
62 Humiliate
63 Big Apple neighborhood
64 Burgundy or Bordeaux
65 "Spider-Man" star Maguire
66 Threesome . . . or a hint to this puzzle's theme

DOWN

1 Golfer's goal
2 Freezer tray contents
3 Hitchcock thriller set in California
4 Relate, as a story
5 Actress Blake
6 Shade in
7 Tool with a rotating handle
8 Privy to
9 "Stormy Weather" singer Horne
10 Flip-flop, e.g.
11 "The Gift of the Magi" writer
12 "___ for the Misbegotten" (O'Neill play)
13 Tears apart
21 Toy you can do tricks with
22 Unlikely prom king
23 "There oughta be ___"
24 Island next to Molokai
28 Embarrassing sound when one bends over
29 "Law & Order," e.g.
30 Jaguar or Impala
31 Québec article
35 Lumberjack's tool
36 Path
37 ___ Paulo, Brazil
38 Michelangelo or Rodin
39 "Get a load of ___!"
40 Kernel
41 Jedi's furry friend
42 Cut out, as coupons
43 Desensitize
44 "More! More!"
45 Like a generic brand
46 "Bedazzled" actor Moore
47 Fastener that turns
48 Rome's ___ Fountain
52 Befuddled
53 Yodel's comeback
54 Run ___ (drink on credit)
55 Give the heave-ho
59 Hawaiian tuna
60 Yoo-___ (chocolate drink)

by Andrea Carla Michaels

14

ACROSS

1 With 74-Across, voting system that affords anonymity . . . or the theme of this puzzle?
7 Game in which the orange ghost is named Sue, not Clyde
15 "Seinfeld" woman
16 Heated disputes
17 Song sung by a patriotic politician
19 Jungle swinger
20 F.D.R. or L.B.J.: Abbr.
21 Vice president Gore and others
22 And others, for short
25 Stridex target, informally
27 Blue stone
31 Singer Damone
33 ___ Party
35 Old Italian coin
36 How a director of campaign advertising works
41 Sought-after rock
42 Rap's Dr. ___
43 However, briefly
44 Turn-___
45 Exactly . . . like a conservative's plan to lower taxes?
49 Possible cause of brain freeze
50 It's seen off la côte de la France
51 Subject of many a political scandal
52 Rooms in una casa
54 ___ Mahal
56 College org. with a Color Guard
59 The Cowboys, on scoreboards
61 React with extreme disgust
63 Louis XIV, e.g.

65 Religious belief of eight U.S. presidents
71 Like no stone, for the meticulous
72 Grand ___ Island
73 Nuisance that keeps returning, in metaphor
74 See 1-Across

DOWN

1 Genesis maker
2 Alter altar plans, maybe
3 Space ___
4 Tease
5 Blowup: Abbr.
6 Cheesed (off)
7 James Stewart title character who goes to Washington
8 ___ Na Na
9 Mountain cat
10 "Does that ring ___?"
11 Event in which you may drive a hard bargain?
12 Hosp. test
13 "This Week" airer
14 Intelligence org.
18 "___ who?!"
23 Bird: Prefix
24 Fancy chocolatier
26 Choppers
28 Assign, as blame
29 Memorable 2011 hurricane
30 Mouthing off
32 PC insert
34 Hearth residue
36 London mayor Johnson
37 Writer Jong
38 German philosopher who wrote "The true is the whole"
39 Fundamental belief

40 One on the way up
46 "Fore!"
47 "Julius Caesar," for one
48 Kitchen brand
53 Buffalo player
55 Pickle holder
57 What a plea bargain obviates
58 Vogue competitor, for short
60 Loretta who sang "Coal Miner's Daughter"
62 Pop's Brothers ___
64 "___ my wit's end"
65 Darts venue
66 Biol. class topic
67 Tarmac fig.
68 Number of years between censuses
69 Like some baseball teams
70 Senators' org.

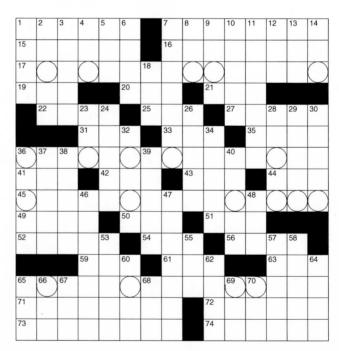

by Erik Agard

ACROSS

1 Automaker with the slogan "Born from jets"
5 Wee hour
8 Fazes
14 Israel's first representative to the United Nations
16 Far from klutzy
17 Nonsensical syllables, maybe
18 They may be followed by trains
19 French place of learning
20 Reynolds who sang "Tammy"
22 Bris or baptism
23 Unbeatable hand
27 Part of a 23-Across
29 Find a tenant for
30 Educ. supporter
31 Elite military group
35 Phaser setting
36 Like the Capitol
37 Wee, to Burns
38 Revealing beachwear
39 So-called "albatross"
40 Sport for high jumpers?
42 Some appliances
43 Bestow, to Burns
44 Arctic explorer John
45 Some Caribbean percussion
49 Superboy's sweetie
53 Nap in Nogales
54 Madison Ave. figure
55 Sicilian smoker
58 Something to sing . . . or a hint to 17-, 23-, 31-, 40- and 45-Across's starts
60 For mature audiences, say
61 Like some compact discs
62 Jeans measure
63 On Soc. Sec., often
64 Methods

DOWN

1 Something that may be rattled
2 Early adders
3 Prior's superior
4 Flavorings for some stews
5 Not yet filled: Abbr.
6 Well-hidden fellow of children's books
7 Well-pitched
8 Acts the dilettante
9 Floating aimlessly
10 Archangel of the Apocrypha
11 Signal approval
12 Reason for a 10th inning
13 Luke, John and others: Abbr.
15 Season after printemps
21 Many a love song
23 Object in court
24 Sinclair who wrote "The Jungle"
25 Smarted
26 Pal around (with)
28 Charisse of "Silk Stockings"
31 Large combo
32 Tickle the funny bone
33 Glacial ridges
34 With 56-Down, "The Joy Luck Club" author
35 Statute that protects journalists' sources
36 Follows persistently
38 Dam agcy.
40 Pistol, for one
41 Form letters?
43 Baum's good witch
46 Lauder of cosmetics
47 Out-and-out
48 1984 Olympic slalom champ Phil
50 Resort isle near Curaçao
51 Hockey great Cam
52 Some recesses
54 Crunch targets
55 CAT scan alternative
56 See 34-Down
57 Sci-fi figures
59 Do lunch

by George Fitzgerald and Nancy Salomon

ACROSS

1 One-named soccer legend
5 "Holy guacamole!"
9 Gary Oldman or Paul Newman
14 Plow animals
15 It's a long story
16 Sound over a subway's public address system, e.g.
17 City with a boardwalk on Monterey Bay
19 Retail activity
20 Online messages
21 Candy from a dispenser
22 Florida theme park
23 Viewing point at the Grand Canyon
25 Fabric fluff
27 General Motors sedan
34 "Yabba dabba ___!"
35 Sicilian volcano
36 Hand on deck
37 Rombauer who wrote "Joy of Cooking"
39 Choose, with "for"
41 Took care of, as bills
42 Do a slow burn
45 Radon or radium: Abbr.
48 12th graders: Abbr.
49 Vacation on the Caribbean, maybe
52 Kind of testimony
53 Thick ___ brick
54 "Beau ___"
57 Mekong Valley native
60 Arctic home
64 Fashion designer Perry
65 Chain gangs, e.g.
67 San Antonio mission
68 One-named New Age singer
69 Poet ___ St. Vincent Millay
70 Poe bird
71 Phone-to-phone communication
72 "Calm down!"

DOWN

1 Sit for a photo
2 Typical semester finish
3 Olin of "Enemies, a Love Story"
4 Total
5 Emergency PC key
6 "The World According to ___"
7 Fever fit
8 Bowl over
9 Failure to appear
10 Mumbo-jumbo
11 Powder on a puff
12 Cookie that can be readily stacked
13 One of the R's of R&R
18 See 26-Down
24 1980s actor with a mohawk
26 With 18-Down, exclamation in "Frankenstein"
27 Jazz pianist Chick
28 Four-bagger
29 Singer Yoko
30 Place for a flag pin
31 Bay State sch.
32 Congo, formerly
33 Termini
34 Tiddlywink or Frisbee
38 Never
40 Pampering, for short
43 Gets a job
44 Little ___, who sang "Do the Loco-Motion with me"
46 Memorable time
47 The "M" of MTV
50 Completely wrong
51 "Amen!"
54 Tent, sleeping bag, hiking shoes, etc.
55 Scat queen Fitzgerald
56 Eastern European
58 Top-flight
59 African antelope
61 Helen of Troy's mother
62 Holds the deed to
63 "The Star-Spangled Banner" opener
66 Krazy ___

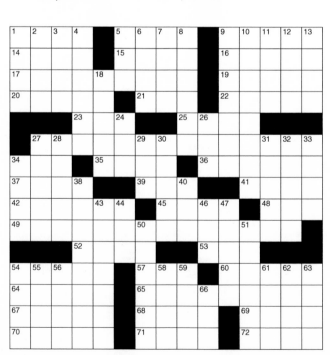

by Randall J. Hartman

ACROSS

1 Blends
6 Sox rival
10 Tiffany collectible
14 Walrus-skin boat
15 Baldwin of "30 Rock"
16 Chapters in history
17 Like some amusement park rides
18 They're sometimes mixed
20 Saxophonist with the 12x platinum album "Breathless"
22 "Seriously!"
23 Vote in favor
24 Dust busters, for short
27 The Evita of "Evita"
28 Father Damien's island
30 Angry Birds, e.g., in 2010
32 Repeated Michael Jackson lyric in a 1987 hit
35 Neighbor of Iraq: Abbr.
36 Many a Bob Marley fan
38 Wasted
39 "___ Man Answers" (1962 film)
40 Blackened (in)
41 Plenty of, casually
42 Talk and talk
43 Final approval
44 Outside: Prefix
45 Disconnects, as a Web address
47 Mah-jongg draws
50 N.F.L. Hall-of-Famer Yale ___
51 "You betcha!"
54 Decorated, say
56 Current measure
58 Calvin Klein perfume
61 Mirage, maybe

62 Comics shrieks
63 Edit command
64 Sweater style
65 Teetotalers
66 Worker with a lot of stress?
67 Maureen Dowd piece

DOWN

1 Like some perfume
2 Host a roast, e.g.
3 Jungle vine
4 "Phooey!"
5 Spirit in a blue bottle
6 Bottleneck
7 "Dark" quaff
8 Elusive legend
9 Dish made with garlic butter
10 "The Merry Widow" composer
11 "Black Swan" director Darren
12 Steeps in a liquid with herbs and spices
13 "Hey!"
19 Start to peak?
21 Guy's partner
25 Back up, as a loan
26 2012 Bond film . . . or a hint to six other Down answers in this puzzle
28 Provides with personnel
29 Oil-rich region
31 Joint groove
32 Goofing off
33 Nickname for Reggie Jackson
34 Busybody
36 Investing all one's money in a penny stock, say
37 Santa ___ (hot winds)
45 Depletes
46 Big inits. for hunters
48 Good earth
49 Triage areas, briefly
51 Toadies' responses
52 ___ Kane, Susan Lucci's Emmy-winning role
53 Like a mosquito
54 Broke ground?
55 Green critter in the Sinclair gas logo
57 Nasty reviews
59 Lofty tribute
60 "That's ___ funny!"

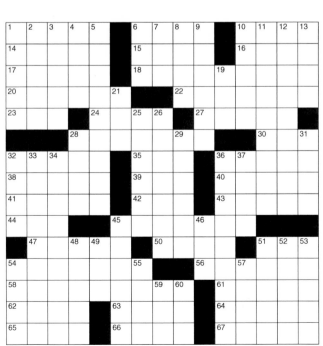

by Don Gagliardo and Zhouqin Burnikel

18

ACROSS

1 Excited, informally
6 Katey of "Married . . . With Children"
11 What a clock checker might want to know, in brief
14 Jazzman Chick
15 Science suffix
16 Chit
17 Aid for skipping out of school?
19 Physics unit
20 What opens and closes safes?
21 "Try ___"
22 "If only"
24 Susan of "The Partridge Family"
25 Sharp-edged plant growth?
28 Blabber's opposite
30 Connect with
31 Dutifully reverent
33 Actress Suvari, co-star of "American Pie"
34 "Jeepers!"
38 Herbal drink
40 Allies of the Cheyenne
42 Emphatic Spanish assent
43 Rockets' paths
45 1950s coup victim
46 Opera ___
48 Did 80, say
49 Shipment of noisemakers, e.g.?
53 Running back's stat: Abbr.
56 "You win"
57 Novelist Morrison
58 One shooting the breeze?
59 "___ your lip!"
60 Area of town where the supernatural hang out?
64 Final letter
65 Up to
66 Auto-racing family name
67 Y : Spanish :: ___ : English
68 Daft
69 First Top 40 hit for Weird Al Yankovic

DOWN

1 Needed a massage, say
2 State animal of Maine
3 Prisoners who write tediously?
4 Reggae's ___-A-Mouse
5 A previous time
6 "Same goes for me"
7 Spaghetti specification
8 Mount Olympus dweller
9 Bio figure
10 Apollo, for one, musically speaking
11 Children's song refrain
12 Arms flank it
13 Zero
18 Tapestry-making device
23 Shout of exuberance
26 "Tony n' ___ Wedding"
27 Wine bottle datum
29 Minstrels, often
31 U.K. V.I.P.'s
32 First Super Bowl that was actually called a Super Bowl
33 Santa ___
35 Robust religious observance?
36 Old unit of conductance
37 In the distance
39 Dodge bullet dodger
41 Sewn-on decoration
44 Traditional family vacation
47 Quite the looker
48 D.C. 100: Abbr.
49 Something delivered in a box
50 Not native
51 Cordoned (off)
52 With faux shyness
54 Words before ask or suggest
55 Comic strip canine
61 "I'll take that as ___"
62 Skater Midori
63 Italian article

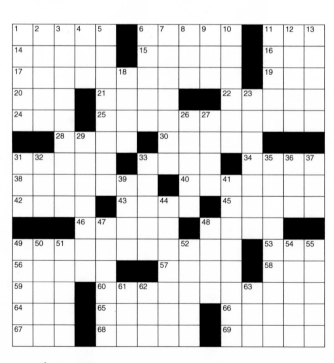

by Joe DiPietro

ACROSS

1 Now: Sp.
6 CD-___
9 Catholic service
13 Plácido Domingo, for one
14 Suffix with Benedict
15 Turn back to zero
16 "My little ___" (W. C. Fields phrase)
18 Perfectly pitched, musically
19 "This is bad!"
20 Boston N.B.A. team
22 Roman philosopher who originated the phrase "What fools these mortals be"
24 Broncobuster
28 "Your" of yesteryear
29 Serious drug cases, for short
31 Actress Zadora
32 Animal high on the evolutionary ladder
33 Toyota make
35 Dangerous dog
37 Lazy
41 St. ___, Caribbean isle
42 With anger
43 Long in the tooth
44 Bon ___ (witticism)
47 Cyberaddress
48 Mil. address
51 New York City suburb near Yonkers
54 Batted body part
56 Strong-smelling cleaner
58 French miss: Abbr.
59 ___ scheme
62 "I Heart ___" (2004 film)
64 Sierra Nevada resort
65 Spanish doubloon material
66 Bricks that click
67 Janis's spouse, in the comics

68 V : five :: X : ___
69 TD Garden, for the 20-Across, e.g.

DOWN

1 For the price of production
2 Cynical laugh
3 Like bialys and lyonnaise sauce
4 Pharmaceutical giant that makes Tamiflu
5 Noah's vessel
6 Merry-go-round, e.g.
7 16 oz.
8 Get together (with)
9 Intelligence group?
10 Query
11 "Get it?"
12 Hog's home
15 Early Elvis Presley style

17 First national park east of the Mississippi
21 Here, to Héloïse
23 Nutso
25 Pro ___ (proportionately)
26 G.M. German car
27 Above, to Francis Scott Key
30 Turf
33 Physics, for one: Abbr.
34 "I don't think so"
36 Like some stares . . . or stairs in the winter
37 Doozy
38 "For Those About to Rock We Salute You" band
39 Promise in a poker pot
40 Winning or losing series

41 Auction unit
45 Electrical unit
46 1980 Kool & the Gang hit
48 Make a claim
49 Add excessive criticism
50 Texas or Ukraine city
52 Instrument for the musically inept, maybe
53 Harden (to)
55 Dying fireplace bit
57 Gateway Arch, for St. Louis, e.g.
59 School fund-raising grp.
60 Boat propeller
61 Blackhawks' org.
63 Pie ___ mode

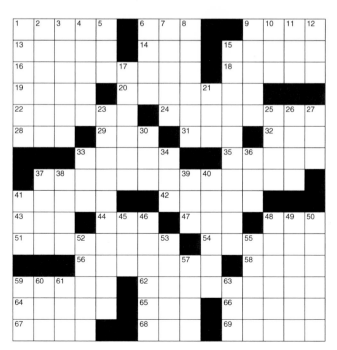

by Paul Guttormsson

ACROSS

1. ___ pants
6. Voting alliance
10. Boxer Riddick
14. Director De Palma
15. Flying: Prefix
16. Nadir's opposite
17. Quite cold
18. Skateboard park feature
19. Left in
20. Provision for ending many a mortgage
23. 2011 Huffington Post purchaser
24. Sergeants major, e.g.: Abbr.
25. Amuse
30. Where Noah made landfall
34. Big Ten football powerhouse, for short
35. Aircraft with pontoons
37. Quite unoriginal
40. Eye, poetically
41. Thread of a screw, e.g.
42. 1970 Freda Payne hit
45. L.A. winter hours
46. Snowmobile brand
47. Google queries
50. Flying fish-eaters
52. Go after
53. Weekend publication since 1941
60. Pig's tail feature
61. MS-DOS alternative
62. Late-night coffee, maybe
63. Helen Crump Taylor's TV stepson
64. Salinger heroine
65. All thumbs
66. Pier
67. Favorable tournament position
68. ___ Kefauver, 1956 vice-presidential candidate

DOWN

1. Former N.Y.C. club
2. ___ 51 (ufologist's interest)
3. Hard-to-take person
4. Vituperate
5. ___ plumbing
6. Home for an owl, maybe
7. Bound
8. Financial adviser Suze
9. Mimic
10. Common fundraiser
11. Unreserved
12. Boohooed
13. Business card abbr.
21. Count ___, character in the Lemony Snicket books
22. Transform (into)
25. TV/radio host Lou
26. Chris with the 1991 hit "Wicked Game"
27. Islam's largest denomination
28. Jam up
29. Pamplona runners
31. Sampson of the 1980s–'90s N.B.A.
32. Biscotti flavoring, sometimes
33. Pastors' readings
36. Qualified
38. Cannonball of jazz fame
39. Irish lullaby syllables
43. Melted-cheese dishes
44. Deputy ___ (Terrytoons character)
48. One who sets the stage?
49. Deceives
51. Rationality
53. ___ platter
54. La Scala presentation
55. Marcel Marceau, for one
56. Got rid of
57. Rapper who co-starred in "Ricochet"
58. Scruff
59. Small salamanders
60. ___ au vin

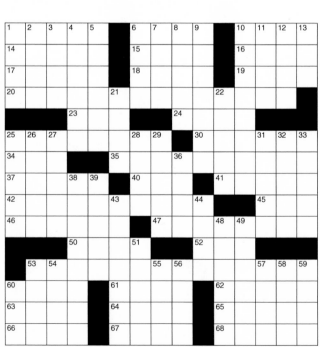

by Allan E. Parrish

21

ACROSS

1 Atypical
4 Bit
9 Ballet dips
14 Once called
15 Skater Sonja
16 Station wagon rear door feature
17 Fraternity letter
18 Open courts
19 Light on one's feet
20 Kind of party
21 German "never"
22 TV drama featuring Ted Danson as D. B. Russell
24 MS. enclosure
25 Maddens
27 Submits
29 "Three Men in ___" ("Our Gang" short)
30 Popular perfume
32 Golfer McIlroy who won the 2011 U.S. Open
33 Starts over, in a way
36 Good-looker
38 Short rebuke
39 Items in a personnel director's in-box
41 ___ Jordan, real name of the Green Lantern
44 Grand ___
45 Israeli, e.g.
47 Snow ___
50 Paucity
52 ___ Candy, "Wonder Woman" character
53 Strange things
55 What circles in a Venn diagram do
58 Network with more than 900 stations
59 Party person?: Abbr.
60 Straightaway
61 Distant
62 Out-and-out
64 Sore, and more
66 ___-goat

67 "Hey Jude" vis-à-vis "Revolution," e.g.
68 Man-___
69 Leoni of "Tower Heist"
70 Set designer's interest
71 Orchestra grouping
72 Byelorussia, e.g.: Abbr.

DOWN

1 2003 Celine Dion album
2 Periods of de-escalation, perhaps
3 U.S. secretary of state tied for the second-longest time in office
4 Former tennis star Michael
5 Fix, as laces
6 Rioting
7 Early 11th-century year
8 Person likely to have a good tan
9 Bagel choice
10 Audio problem
11 "Yes"
12 Patisserie treat
13 Lustrous
23 Pan-fries
26 Five-spot
28 Like some wit
31 ___ accent, mark used symmetrically six times in this puzzle's solution
34 Sample
35 Hand-holding event
37 Indianapolis-to-Cincinnati dir.
40 More deserving of an R rating, say
41 Targets appear on them

42 Some cases
43 2012, for one
44 33rd prez
46 Outlet for une rivière
47 Basketball squad, e.g.
48 Piece of hard-hitting journalism
49 ___ valve
51 Fund-raiser's request
54 Thumb twiddler
56 Made an X, maybe
57 Servers at some restaurants
63 Stir
65 "Norma ___"

by David J. Kahn

22

ACROSS
1 Dull-colored
5 Financial reserves for later years, in brief
9 Von ___ family ("The Sound of Music" group)
14 Wife of Charlie Chaplin
15 Top of the Capitol
16 Floor machine
17 Fish propellers
18 Of a church flock
19 Chilling, as Champagne
20 Pancakes
23 Firmament
24 What a barber must cut around
25 Escargot
27 Wee-hours periods, for short
30 Salsa or guacamole
32 Denigrates
36 Rolaids competitor
38 Chaz's mother
40 Spooky
41 Waffles
44 Rarely visited room
45 Western alliance since 1949
46 One of 18 on a golf course
47 Reason for a 10th inning, say
49 Finish
51 Feb. follower
52 Large amounts of bacon
54 Walton of Walmart
56 Ave. intersectors
59 French toast
64 Bananalike fruit
66 Algerian port
67 Give everyone a hand
68 Wahine's greeting
69 F sharp major and others
70 Bordeaux buddies

71 Change the price on
72 Popeye's ___' Pea
73 Distinctive Marilyn Monroe facial feature

DOWN
1 Remove, as a hat
2 Stir up
3 She was the "I" in "The King and I"
4 Moisten, as a turkey
5 Leisure class
6 Horse color
7 Not quite right
8 Inferior
9 Cheated on, romantically
10 Sought office
11 Line of rotation
12 Amount for Peter Piper

13 Rabbits, to eagles, e.g.
21 Wee bit
22 Dubai's federation: Abbr.
26 Bloodsucker
27 Up, in baseball
28 Prefix with task
29 Struck down, biblically
31 Obsolescent directories
33 Virginia Woolf's "___ of One's Own"
34 Nabisco's ___ wafers
35 Passover supper
37 Big swallows
39 Greek vowel
42 Scamp
43 Gobbledygook
48 Dallas cager, for short
50 "Law & Order" figs.

53 Scatter, as seeds
55 "___, I'm Adam"
56 Trade punches in training
57 Scheherazade offering
58 Good name for a Dalmatian
60 Funny Martha of old TV
61 Pixar's "Finding ___"
62 Homophone for 57-Down
63 "If all ___ fails . . ."
65 "I see it now!"

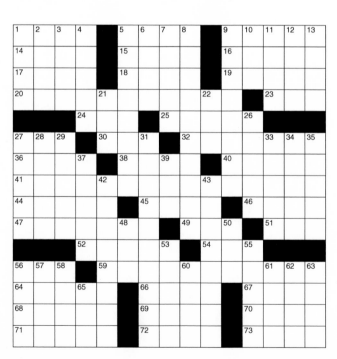

by Ed Sessa

ACROSS

1 ___ Sea (inland body with high salinity)
5 With 67-Across, song by 56-Across
9 Sword part
13 Radius, e.g.
14 Comic strip dog with a long tongue
15 Spine-tingling
16 Lash
17 Ike's partner in 1960s–'70s music
18 Bicycle shorts material
19 With 32-Across, song by 56-Across
22 Half a school year: Abbr.
23 Chaos
24 Splinter group
26 Rat-___
28 Conveyance in an Ellington song
32 See 19-Across
37 Pres. Carter's alma mater
38 Having throbbing temples, maybe
39 Fourth notes
40 Expensive
41 Actress Taylor of "Six Feet Under"
42 Song by 56-Across
44 City SSW of Seattle
46 Peacekeeping grp.
47 Afternoon refreshers
49 Long rant
53 London-based record label
56 Musician born 11/27/42
59 "Deliverance" instrument
61 Panache
62 Lickety-split, in a memo
63 Passion

64 Pete and Julie's "Mod Squad" partner
65 Job for an actor
66 Where to buy GM and GE
67 See 5-Across
68 Compound with a double-bonded carbon atom

DOWN

1 Former sitcom on the Beeb
2 "Good Times" actress Esther
3 "You can't teach ___ dog . . ."
4 Lawsuit
5 Bygone company with yellow-roofed kiosks
6 Thor's father
7 RR ___
8 "A Full Moon in March" poet
9 With 60-Down, song by 56-Across
10 Three-point lines in basketball, e.g.
11 Song by 56-Across
12 Word after mule or school
15 Choose
20 Tool that turns
21 Catch, in a way
25 Sleepover game, maybe
27 Sukiyaki ingredient
29 Where sailors go
30 1966 hurricane
31 A ponytail hangs over it
32 What picked flowers may do
33 Prima donna's delivery
34 After-bath powder

35 Card game for two
36 "Pardon the Interruption" airer
40 Arrive, as darkness
42 Big ___ (baseball's David Ortiz)
43 Period of inactivity
45 Biology or English
48 What bloodhounds and dead fish do
50 Bad ignition?
51 Connect with an operator
52 Kick out
53 Abba of Israel
54 "The Wind Cries ___" (song by 56-Across)
55 Neither Dems. nor Reps.
57 Hip parts
58 13 cards, maybe
60 See 9-Down

by Peter A. Collins

24

ACROSS

1 Goose egg
6 "Major" beast
10 Porter's regretful Miss
14 From Basra, say
15 Time to stuff stockings
16 [sigh]
17 Start of an algebra problem
20 Toby filler
21 To __ (perfectly)
22 Heating option
23 Least fresh
27 Throw one's support behind
29 "__ nerve!"
30 Poet with a "fanatic's heart"
32 Passage preventers, often
33 Québec assent
34 Jettison
35 Outgoing flight stat
36 The rest of the algebra problem
41 Kitty
42 "L'__ c'est moi"
43 Alternative to Yahoo!
45 It has feathers and flies
47 Black Sabbath's genre
49 Benchmarks: Abbr.
50 Think tank types
52 Like stir-fry
54 Meditation sounds
55 One-in-a-million
57 Messenger __
58 Answer to the algebra problem
64 Steaming
65 Causes of some celebrity clashes
66 Link with
67 Fictional Flanders and Devine

68 Kind of day for a competitive cyclist
69 Historic English county

DOWN

1 Beiderbecke of jazz
2 Dadaist Jean
3 Guy's mate
4 Regard as identical
5 Fine cotton thread
6 Prefix with -form
7 Parks in front of a bus?
8 Sonnet part
9 Xenophobes' fear
10 Muesli morsel
11 Mrs. Robinson's movie
12 "Fine with me"
13 Classic quintet
18 Response to "Who, me?"

19 Marked, in a way
23 Menu general
24 Gumbo thickener
25 "Wow!"
26 Actress Harper of "No Country for Old Men"
28 Savvy about
31 Until now
34 Cause of a boom and bust?
35 Young newt
37 Smidge
38 "Take __ a sign"
39 Subject of a cap, in sports
40 Didn't go by foot
44 "Dropped" drug
45 Compound in Agent Orange
46 Venerate
47 More Scrooge-like
48 Tee off

49 Equilibrium
51 Battlefield fare: Abbr.
53 Pull together
56 Slaughter in baseball
59 Some highlight reel features, for short
60 Summer hrs.
61 Parisian's possessive
62 Ore suffix
63 Affectionate sign-off

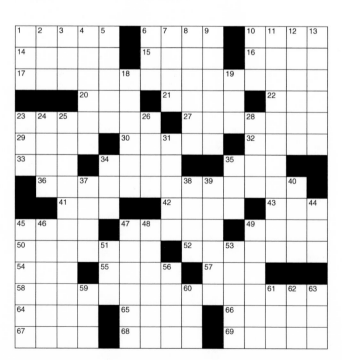

by Adam G. Perl

ACROSS

1 Dacha or villa
6 Rock used to make sparks
11 Equine : horse :: vulpine : ___
14 Unsophisticated sorts
15 Storm tracker
16 Dined
17 End-of-semester doings
18 With 61-Across, goal of Frederick Douglass and Harriet Beecher Stowe
20 Big book
21 Disclosure to a loan applicant: Abbr.
22 U.S. capital and environs
23 With 51-Across, presidential order signed on January 1, 1863
26 Hit it off with
27 Old Russian leaders
31 Art movement for Picasso
34 Scrooge player Alastair
36 Stockyard call
37&39 Signer of the 23-/51-Across
42 Jetsam locale
43 Rapper with the #1 album "Hip Hop Is Dead"
45 Almost
46 ___-Detoo of "Star Wars"
49 Signs of spring
51 See 23-Across
56 Acquired with little or no effort
59 TV's Sue ___ Langdon
60 Romance
61 See 18-Across
63 "Holy Toledo!"
64 "It's f-f-freezing!"
65 Salsa singer Cruz

66 Lectern
67 Jazz style
68 Rickover known as the Father of the Nuclear Navy
69 Imbeciles

DOWN

1 Mountain ridge
2 Big-bosomed
3 Time's Person of the Year for 2008 and 2012
4 Loss of faculties
5 Beginning of summer?
6 Fruity iced beverage
7 Runners of experiments
8 Nuptial vow
9 Old-time actress Nita
10 Knit fabric in lingerie and swimwear
11 Like a fly ball off the foul pole

12 Tribe encountered by Lewis and Clark
13 Lucy Lawless title role
19 Bronzes
21 Quarterback Troy
24 Legal tender
25 Labor
28 Omnia vincit ___
29 Move on casters
30 LG Electronics competitor
31 House in Havana
32 Above, in Berlin
33 Misbehaver
35 Role for diminutive Verne Troyer in "Austin Powers" films
38 Artist Chagall
40 "99 Luftballons" singer, 1984
41 Made a random selection, in a way

44 Sunny rooms
47 German automaker
48 Jerry of stage and screen
50 Canopy tree
52 Comment from a kvetcher
53 Early Great Plains residents
54 Sheeplike
55 Imperatives
56 All-time career batting average leader
57 Early Michael Jackson hairstyle
58 Car sticker fig.
62 Tree in many street names
63 When doubled, a Gabor

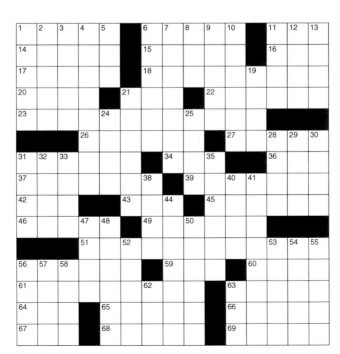

by John Farmer

26

ACROSS

1 Spooky
6 Walk with heavy steps
11 College transcript no.
14 What a cowboy may use while saying "Giddyup!"
15 Course to breeze through
16 Brit. resource for wordsmiths
17 Inspector Clouseau movie, with "The"
19 Hi-fi supply
20 "If I Had a Hammer" singer Lopez
21 Rye and whole wheat
23 Invent, as a phrase
24 TV host Philbin
27 Stats for sluggers
29 Air that makes you go [cough, cough]
30 Alert to danger
31 Martial arts actor Lee
32 Asian New Year
33 Draped Delhi dress
34 Start a Web session
35 Poet Gelett Burgess wrote that he never saw one
38 Bitterly pungent
41 Gentle rise and fall of the voice
42 Ghost's cry
45 Plodding journeys
46 Emperor who fiddled around?
47 Like the models in a swimsuit issue
48 Pie à la ___
49 Patients, to doctors
50 What you might catch a tiger by, in a saying
51 Pull out
53 Antelope with a hump and twisted horns

55 "How was ___ know?"
56 Lewis Carroll character who's late
60 Politico ___ Paul
61 Belly button
62 Public square
63 Unspecified amount
64 Take furtively
65 Rocker Bob with the Silver Bullet Band

DOWN

1 Parapsychology subject, briefly
2 Perfect example
3 Go wild
4 Annoying
5 Jock's channel
6 Number of sides in a decagon
7 Squealer
8 Rubbish holder
9 Fort ___, Fla.

10 Cut, as expenses
11 Edgar Allan Poe story, with "The"
12 Its brands include Frito-Lay and Tropicana
13 Commercials
18 Combat with fighter-bombers
22 Symbol by the phrase "You are here"
23 Chicago's winter hrs.
25 O.K. Corral gunslinger
26 Decorative gratings
28 One of 100 on the Hill: Abbr.
31 Ink stain
33 Soapy froth
35 Cheapskate
36 Yeats's homeland
37 Ninth-inning relief pitcher

38 Source of PIN money?
39 Salad cube
40 John Steinbeck book, with "The"
42 Hacky Sack, basically
43 Form rust, say
44 Popeye's Olive ___
46 Indigenous
47 Sty : hogs :: ___ : horses
49 George M. who composed "Over There"
52 Holds the title to
54 Swimmers' distances
55 Money for the senior yrs.
57 Afternoon social
58 Antlered animal
59 Black goo

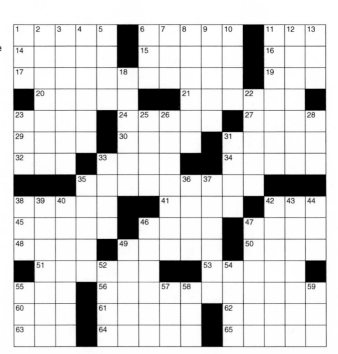

by Lynn Lempel

ACROSS

1 Loss of heart
7 Mardi Gras wear
11 Go for it
14 "Seinfeld" woman
15 Prefix with potent
16 Go fast
17 Prison for soda jerks?
19 Simile center
20 When prompted
21 Proofer's mark
22 MapQuest suggestions: Abbr.
23 "What's Going On" singer Marvin
24 Prison for bishops?
26 La-la lead-in
28 Patches, as a fairway
29 Sweep's heap
32 Modern means of relaying jokes
36 Shut down
39 Prison for vintners?
42 Islamic equivalent of kosher
43 Bandleader Skinnay ___
44 Part of a journey
45 Lady of the Haus
47 10-digit no.
49 Prison for corny humorists?
54 Ayatollah's land
58 Has
59 Melt ingredient
60 Cartoon art genre
61 A fire sign
62 Prison for gardeners?
64 Doc with a tongue depressor, maybe
65 Creole cooking pod
66 "Good comeback!"
67 Draft org.
68 Call for
69 Slow movers

DOWN

1 Clear up, as a windshield
2 Massey of old films
3 Smart-mouthed
4 Stately dance in ¾ time
5 It may be upped
6 Roll-call call
7 "Haystacks" artist Claude
8 More than enough
9 Shows derision
10 Thanksgiving guests, often
11 "Over and out"
12 Affected by 13-Down
13 Bakery supply
18 Infamous Amin
22 Its competitors may be thrown
24 Singer Michelle or Cass
25 Full of merriment
27 Slo-mo footage, perhaps
29 Oktoberfest "Oh!"
30 Doo-wop group ___ Na Na
31 Macramé ties
33 Census datum
34 Travel guide listing
35 Spy novelist Deighton
37 "Didn't I tell you?"
38 Fraction of a joule
40 Horses that produce milk
41 Nancy in France, e.g.
46 Slow on the ___
48 ___ franca
49 They may be punched
50 1936 Olympics star Jesse
51 Bizarre
52 Work, as dough
53 The "E" in 64-Across
55 Christina of "Monster"
56 Menotti title role
57 Spanish babies
60 Like most bathroom graffiti: Abbr.
62 Took the cake
63 "___ been real!"

by Jeffrey Wechsler

28

ACROSS

1 Revenue / Result
6 Many a holiday visitor / Bandit
10 Welcome, as a visitor / Try to make a date with
14 Comedian George
15 1980s Geena Davis sitcom
16 Locale for a seat of honor
17 1985 Kate Nelligan title role
18 Chickadee's perch
19 Up to the job
20 Condor's claw
21 College asset
23 Glean
25 Oldest U.S. civil liberties org.
26 At a lecture, say / Surpass in quality
29 Steel helmets with visors
34 Daughter of 28-Down
35 Genesis victim
37 Gawk
38 Priest's garb
39 Choice for a dog, as well as a hint to this puzzle's theme
41 Half a score
42 Has rolling in the aisles
44 Trick ending?
45 Gist
46 Lacking inflection
48 Sub / Excel
50 D.C. bigwig
51 False god
52 Grand Canyon material
57 Doritos dip
61 "Uh-huh"
62 What a surveyor surveys
63 Govt. security
64 ___ Bora, wild part of Afghanistan

65 The Box Tops' "___ Her in Church"
66 Painter's prop
67 Soon to get / Trying to get
68 Ushered / Showed the door
69 Attract / Protract

DOWN

1 Fjord / Bargain locale
2 Mixer
3 Autobahn auto
4 Holiday display
5 Periodicals not brought by a postal carrier
6 Foot part / Go beyond
7 White House adjunct
8 Parched
9 They may be covered and circled
10 Unwavering
11 Kemo ___
12 Brick baker
13 Map feature / Start
22 Watch location
24 ___ example
26 Arriving at the tail end / Survive
27 It has four strings
28 Brother of Rebecca, in the Bible
29 Some Muppet dolls
30 Burn balm
31 Consumed
32 Tire feature
33 Submitted, as an entry / Emitted
36 Honcho
39 Antilles, e.g.
40 ___ Major
43 Spouse's response

45 India's ___ Coast
47 Necessitate
49 Tried
51 Hit so as to make collapse / Win over
52 '60s protest / Skip, as a dance
53 From
54 Peter at the ivories
55 "It's either you ___"
56 Poverty
58 Marge's TV daughter
59 What Cain did to 35-Across
60 Tired / Total

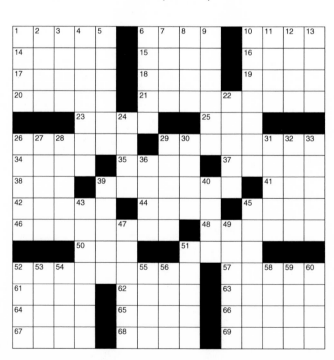

by C. W. Stewart

ACROSS

1 What skunks do
6 Oared racing shell
11 Harley-Davidson, slangily
14 Domed domicile
15 Book after Daniel
16 One-spot
17 "Keep going!"
19 Born: Fr.
20 Workers just for the day
21 Edgar who painted dancers
23 "Sound off – one, two . . .," e.g.
26 Square cracker
28 ___ about (roughly)
29 Neighbor of an Azerbaijani
31 Cheap seat cover material
33 Pizazz
34 Cough medicine amt.
37 Superlative suffix
38 Do impressions of
41 Garden tool
42 "I agree"
43 Donated
44 Erupts
46 Coffee liqueur brand
50 Nabisco cookie
51 Bibliophile
53 Playful puppies
55 Mumbai money
56 Baby food (whose name is an anagram of 55-Across)
57 Hostel
58 "Keep going!"
64 Prefix with tourism
65 Decorative upholstery fabric
66 Acquire information
67 Small number
68 Peevish states
69 Letters before tees

DOWN

1 Use a stool
2 Store head: Abbr.
3 Bridge writer Culbertson
4 Scratch-off game, e.g.
5 Best Actress for "Two Women"
6 Woodworking tool
7 Gear teeth
8 Where Springsteen was born, in song
9 Floral necklace
10 Noncellular phones
11 "Keep going!"
12 Atlantic or Pacific
13 Fliers in V's
18 Village People hit whose title completes the line "It's fun to stay at the . . ."
22 Seventh Greek letter
23 Small flock
24 Licorice-tasting seed
25 "Keep going!"
26 Actress Ward
27 Course related to physiology: Abbr.
30 It might go from 0 to 60 minutes
32 Easily torn bands of tissue
35 Spreader of seeds
36 Mexican money
39 Papa's mate
40 "Terrible" czar
45 Popular chain of chicken restaurants
47 Dick was his running mate in '52 and '56
48 Hardens
49 Broadcasts
51 Succinct
52 1/16 of a pound
54 "Positive thinker" Norman Vincent ___
56 Animal hide
59 Seeming eternity
60 7, to Caesar
61 "___ Rheingold"
62 Wrath
63 Coast Guard officer: Abbr.

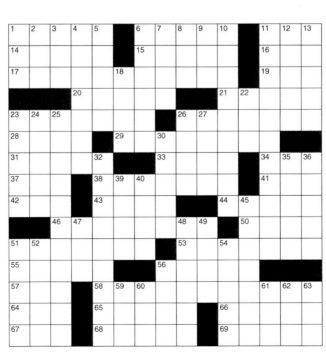

by Betty Keller

ACROSS

1 Org. for boomers, now
5 Smooth-talking
9 Cause of something going up?
14 Iranian money
15 The last Mrs. Charlie Chaplin
16 London line
17 Food-stamping org.
18 Do a cashier's job
19 Tech callers
20 Attack helicopter
22 "___ Lay Dying"
23 Raptor's roost
24 Sister of Rachel
26 Snack machine inserts
29 Abode, informally
31 Do a cashier's job
33 Day-___ colors
34 "Just a ___" (1931 hit)
37 Director Kazan
38 Pick on, in a way
39 WWW bookmark
40 Often-joked-about professionals
42 Summer on the Seine
43 Ellington's "Prelude ___ Kiss"
44 Will-___-wisp
45 Walk unsteadily
47 U.S.N.A. grad
48 Portuguese king
49 Zeus, to the Romans
50 The Big Board, for short
52 Cornell or Pound
54 Make rhapsodic
58 Where to read about the 50-Across: Abbr.
60 In the altogether
62 Gaucho's rope
64 Baseball's Moises

65 "Holy cow!"
66 "Over the Rainbow" composer Harold
67 Lincoln's state: Abbr.
68 Sons of ___ (group promoting Irish heritage)
69 Far from faithful
70 Determination
71 Root beer brand

DOWN

1 Tourist mecca off Venezuela
2 Seating option
3 Weather forecaster's tool
4 Tenor Domingo
5 "Holy cow!"
6 Many subway trains
7 Blown away

8 Sure to bring in money
9 Pastel hue
10 Costner's "Tin Cup" co-star
11 Really steamed
12 Wilder's "___ Town"
13 Classic game console letters
21 Radio host Garrison
25 Buzz, bob or bangs
27 Select few
28 Unloaded?
30 Colonel Sanders facial feature
32 Appliance with a pilot
34 Word before "Morgen" or "Tag"
35 O. Henry literary device
36 See-through partition

37 Word that can follow each half of 20- and 60-Across and 11- and 36-Down
41 Super-duper
46 Stuck in traffic, say
49 Derek of "I, Claudius"
51 ___ Park, Colo.
53 Kaiser or czar
55 Director Kurosawa
56 Not so hot
57 Idyllic spots
59 Girl with the dog Spot
61 Quarterback Warner
62 Luftwaffe foe: Abbr.
63 Portfolio part, for short

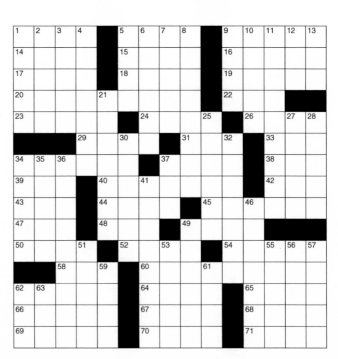

by Thomas Takaro

ACROSS

1 Ohio town called the Bicycle Capital of the Midwest
6 Sitcom father of Mearth
10 Longest-serving senator in U.S. history
14 Sing ___
15 "The ___ Love"
16 Be biased
17 Wedding flower girl, maybe
18 Librarian's imperative
19 It's below the elbow
20 *Bush cabinet member who resigned in 2006
23 Wall Street earnings abbr.
24 Monopoly token
25 ___ Grand
26 *Her "Rehab" won a Grammy for Song of the Year
31 Out
34 Leaves after dinner?
35 Actress Naldi of the silents
36 All day every day
39 Friend from way, way back
41 Opening for outside?
42 Spread
44 Places for hops
45 *Best Actor winner for "The Champ," 1931
49 First P.M. of Burma
50 Proto-matter from which the universe was made
51 Real ending?
54 *"Star Wars" actress who's a Harvard grad
58 New member of la familia

59 Simple quatrain form
60 Al-Qatif, for one
61 ___ Sea, outlet of the Amu Darya
62 Small songbirds
63 New Mexico county
64 Glowing
65 Old pump name
66 Livia, to Tiberius

DOWN

1 2005 #1 album for Coldplay
2 Poet who wrote "This is the way the world ends / Not with a bang but a whimper"
3 Incessantly
4 Ancient Peruvian
5 What some amusement park rides have
6 Rob of "Numb3rs"

7 A pint, typically, at a blood bank
8 Chew out
9 Restaurant offering that might come with a toy
10 1957 Fats Domino hit
11 Holler
12 Pretoria money
13 Strand material
21 Towel off
22 String after E
26 "No doubt!"
27 Prefix with liberal
28 180's
29 Factoid for fantasy baseball
30 "I'm all ___"
31 Fresh
32 "Livin' La Vida ___"
33 Worldwide: Abbr.
37 Kiss

38 "The Bells" writer
40 Stereotypically messy digs
43 "The Second Coming" poet
46 Tennis's Ivanovic
47 City on the Rio Grande
48 Want ad abbr.
51 "No more for me"
52 Congo, once
53 Artist James
54 "I, Claudius" figure
55 "Down with . . . !": Fr.
56 Relative of a stork
57 "Ciao"
58 Judging by their names, where the answers to the four starred clues might be found?

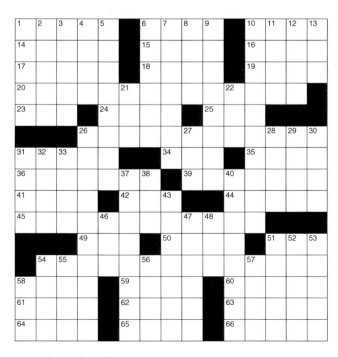

by Caleb Madison

Note: The answers to the eight starred clues all have something in common, each in a different way.

ACROSS

1 China's ___ Zedong
4 ___ and sciences
8 Wrist, elbow and ankle
14 Reach
16 Shook hands (on)
17 *Fraternity with a sweetheart of a song
18 *Drink that often comes with an umbrella
19 Afternoon socials
20 "My bad!"
22 Cold war foe, for short
23 Info on a W-2 form: Abbr.
24 *Like some socks
26 "Après ___ le déluge"
28 Ready for skinny-dipping
29 Rx signers
32 Bryn Mawr graduate
35 Cause of a clock change twice a yr.
36 Paint layer
37 *Smart aleck
39 *Salon supply in a bottle
41 "___ go bragh!"
42 Cold and blustery
44 Attach with Elmer's
45 Cul-de-___
46 "___ Was a Rollin' Stone"
47 "Bad" cholesterol, for short
48 *Good picnic forecast
51 Opposite of post-
54 "The Simpsons" girl
56 Lt. Kojak
57 Plenty
58 *Chocolaty ice cream dessert
60 *Second-generation senator from Indiana

62 Away from the coast
63 Faith
64 Insurance sellers
65 Exam given face-to-face
66 Snaky swimmer

DOWN

1 Sail holders
2 First sign of the zodiac
3 Hymn accompaniment
4 ___ Gardner, Mrs. Sinatra #2
5 Military info-gathering
6 Sierra Nevada resort lake
7 Grad student's income, often
8 Smucker's product
9 Track choice for Lionel trains
10 Like many St. Patrick's Day celebrants
11 Meshes
12 Rip
13 U.S. Star Wars program
15 AOL chitchat
21 "Be quiet!"
24 Queen's mate
25 Dangler on a dog collar
27 Broken mirror, to some
29 Small replica of the Spirit of St. Louis, e.g.
30 Harry Belafonte catchword
31 Brit's W.W. II gun
32 Fills with wonder
33 Franc : France :: ___ : Italy
34 Saintly glows
36 Gunk

38 Talk to persistently and with a big mouth
40 Badly
43 Purple Heart recipient
46 Lament
48 Network showing Capitol Hill proceedings
49 Cut off
50 Australian eucalyptus eater
52 Rolls-___ (car)
53 Jazzy Waters
54 Where inhaled air goes
55 No longer working
57 Lawyers' org.
58 ___ Farrow, Mrs. Sinatra #3
59 Bradley and Begley
61 Zilch

by Lynn Lempel

ACROSS
1 Comprehend
6 Contemptible
10 Shade of many a swimming pool basin
14 Surgeon's tool
15 Web addresses
16 Parts of a tea set
17 Sprightly
18 Politician's goal
19 Give the heave-ho
20 1940s hit radio show featuring the bartender Archie
23 Salad additive
24 Marveled audibly (at)
28 1939 James Joyce novel
33 Second-smallest state: Abbr.
34 Instrument held with two hands
35 Pakistani leader, 1977–88
36 1960s sitcom about a group of castaways
41 G.I. entertainers
42 X ___ xylophone
43 Work unit
44 1946 Bing Crosby hit
49 Blog messages
50 Sculler's item
51 1960s sitcom set in a P.O.W. camp
59 On the briny
62 "Am ___ late?"
63 ___ cotta
64 Wimbledon surface
65 Head for
66 Jew traditionally dressed in a black coat and hat
67 Canned
68 Period of time
69 Solo

DOWN
1 Delighted
2 Prego competitor
3 "Yeah, right!"
4 "To thine own ___ be true"
5 Victimize
6 Ado
7 Geographical datum
8 Czech, e.g., but not a Hungarian
9 Ferrara ruling family
10 Ad exhortation
11 Status ___
12 Good times
13 Numbskull
21 Transgress
22 Kentucky Derby prize
25 Sand trap, e.g.
26 Barely making, with "out"
27 Defunct
28 Prison population
29 Needing a doctor's attention
30 "___ Fly Now" ("Rocky" theme)
31 Tummy muscles
32 "___ won't!"
33 Establishment with a revolving mirrored ball
36 Forrest ___, 1994 Oscar-winning role
37 Schoolyard retort
38 Fed. property overseer
39 Publicize
40 Novelist Deighton
45 Available
46 "Already?"
47 "Rubbish!"
48 First name in soul
52 Play dates?
53 Surmounting
54 ___ bene
55 Down-to-earth
56 Roughly
57 Land that's saluted in this puzzle
58 Marquis de ___
59 Menu phrase
60 Instrument famously played by Bill Clinton on "The Arsenio Hall Show"
61 One catching a ram's eye

by Richard Chisholm

34

ACROSS

1 Parroting sorts
6 Stud on a stud farm
10 Good name, casually
13 Venue for some clowns
14 Word before city or child
15 Basis for some discrimination
16 Mystery desserts?
18 Thing to roll over, in brief
19 East ___, U.N. member since 2002
20 Central part
22 Oscar winner Sorvino
25 Acquired relative
27 Musical with the song "Mr. Mistoffelees"
28 Equal to, with "with"
30 O.K. to do
32 Orange feature
33 Bates's business, in film
35 Video shooter, for short
38 Direction from K.C. to Detroit
39 Stir up
41 ___-Ida (Tater Tots maker)
42 Top end of a scale
43 Miming dances
44 Visibly frightened
46 Bucky Beaver's toothpaste
48 High-hats
49 Soprano Gluck
51 Refrain syllables
54 "Spare me!," e.g.
55 Place for a lark
57 Winter coat feature
59 Diamond corner
60 Sculler's affliction?
65 Time of anticipation
66 First-rate
67 Many an art film
68 ___ judicata
69 Hebrides isle
70 Take as one's own

DOWN

1 Flight board abbr.
2 Samoan staple
3 Byrnes of TV's "77 Sunset Strip"
4 Reason for a long delay in getting approval, maybe
5 Arias, e.g.
6 Motorist's headache
7 Calligrapher's buy
8 Period of seven days without bathing?
9 Gaelic tongue
10 What the sky might do in an inebriate's dream?
11 Everglades denizen
12 Belfry sounds
14 Pic to click
17 Mideast V.I.P.
21 Zenith competitor
22 "Impression, Sunrise" painter
23 Cockamamie
24 Illustrations for a Poe poem?
26 Choir voices
29 Leader of the pack
31 Pick up bit by bit
33 Place for a crown
34 In vitro items
36 Mountain ridge
37 Group with a meeting of the minds?
40 Employment in Munchkinland?
45 Choir voice
47 Inflate, in a way
48 Spilled the beans
49 Honey-hued
50 Take a powder
52 Sitcom with the catchphrase "Kiss my grits!"
53 ___ sausage
56 Tolkien beasts
58 "Beowulf," e.g.
61 Modus operandi
62 Courtroom vow
63 Barely beat
64 The "all" in "Collect them all!"

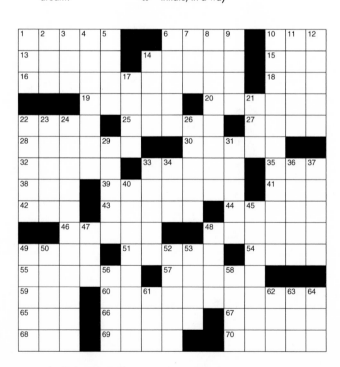

by Robert A. Doll

ACROSS

1 Point the finger at
6 Impudent
10 Jail unit
14 Parts to play
15 One putting finishing touches on a cake
16 Light greenish blue
17 Worker for 15%, say
18 "Meet Me at the __"
19 Japanese wrestling
20 Fix part of dinner with lettuce, carrots, peppers, etc.
22 Large part of a waiter's income
23 A.B.A. member: Abbr.
24 Game company behind Sonic the Hedgehog
26 Play a part
29 Go off like Mount St. Helens
31 Sailor's "Stop!"
35 Writer Harte
37 Put __ good word for
38 Words cried before "No hands!"
39 Activity with bubbles
40 Retail giant selling dog food, birdcages and such
42 Knots
43 Islands west of Portugal
45 __-Magnon man
46 Coup d'__
47 Church council
48 Food Network stars
50 "__ you ready?"
51 Take a 39-Across
53 Boneheads
55 __ California
58 Prepare to camp

63 Minnesota's St. __ College
64 What "video" means literally
65 Bit part
66 Sitarist Shankar
67 In tatters
68 Perrier competitor
69 Pesky flier
70 Lighted sign over a door
71 Bush's 2004 opponent

DOWN

1 Kid with frequent temper tantrums
2 Golden arches, for McDonald's
3 Pub draughts
4 High-I.Q. group
5 Billionaire's home
6 Petty
7 Environmental sci.
8 Meal
9 Swap
10 Participate on Election Day
11 Prefix with lateral
12 It's in your throat when you choke up
13 Vientiane's land
21 Bacon units
25 Fed. auditing agcy.
26 The P.L.O.'s Mahmoud __
27 Touched in the head
28 Wyoming's __ Range
30 Where watermelons grow
32 Japanese dog
33 Mascara mess
34 Important sense for a gourmet
36 Show childish anger

38 Sponge used in a 39-Across
41 Moon shape
44 Psychologist/writer LeShan
48 Longtime Comiskey Park team, informally
49 Sissy of "Carrie"
52 Ill will
54 Prevent, with "off"
55 Tennis's Bjorn
56 Astronaut Shepard or Bean
57 Coffee, slangily
59 Garr or Hatcher
60 Mideast bigwig
61 Close
62 Broadway honor

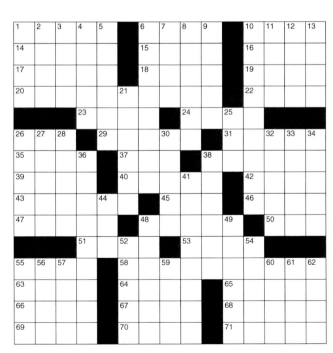

by Randy Sowell

36

ACROSS

1 Wrote an ode to
7 China's Chou En-___
10 Captain Hook's henchman
14 Cause of weird weather
15 Press worker's stain
16 Brighton bye-bye
17 Augments
18 Wine servers
20 Adolescent boy's growth
22 Recurring Woody Allen theme
23 Have a go at
24 What oil helps dissolve
25 "I Pity the Fool" star
26 Brother of Little Joe on '60s TV
27 "Jingle Bells" starter
31 Little green man
34 Soldier's period of service
36 Isaac's eldest
37 Cocoon occupants
38 Little green men, for short
39 Target competitor
40 Where a tab is inserted
41 Joan of the Blackhearts
42 "Biography" network, once
43 King Cole was a merry one
45 "Death in Venice" author Thomas
47 Demolition aid
48 "The Witches" director Nicolas
49 Some Super Bowl Sunday highlights
52 Africa's largest city
55 Bargains for leniency
57 Dukakis in 1988 and Dole in 1996
59 (0,0) on a graph

60 Reach a high
61 Grampa Simpson
62 They can be found in 20- and 55-Across and 10- and 26-Down
63 Lap dog, informally
64 Window units, briefly
65 Electrician's alloy

DOWN

1 Did an axel, e.g.
2 Tree with catkins
3 It's observed on Oct. 24
4 Wink in tiddlywinks, e.g.
5 Make king or queen
6 Goofball
7 "Hungarian Rhapsodies" composer
8 Animated bug film of 1998
9 Clanton at the O.K. Corral
10 Musial's nickname
11 Helgenberger of "CSI"
12 LAX postings
13 American League division
19 Some are declared
21 J. P. Morgan co.
25 Scratch
26 Dehydration may help bring this on
27 Housecleaning aid
28 "This ___ outrage!"
29 Source of a fragrant oil
30 "___ Nacht" (German words of parting)
31 Lhasa ___
32 Temporary calm
33 Popular MP3 player
35 Mel in Cooperstown

39 Emblem on the Australian coat of arms
41 Protrude
44 ___ about (circa)
46 "___ Fables"
48 Gift on Valentine's Day
49 Chilly
50 Make less chilly
51 Less loopy
52 Al who created Fearless Fosdick
53 Away from the wind
54 "Out of Africa" author Dinesen
55 "Fast Money" network
56 Dosage unit
58 Battery size

by Pancho Harrison

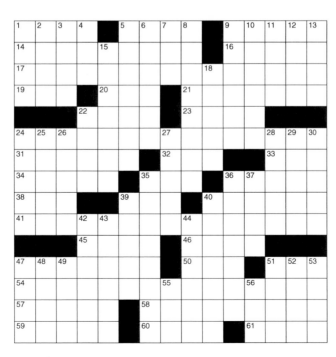

ACROSS
1 Tree trunk
5 Some HDTVs
9 Heartbreaker who's "back in town" in a 1980 Carly Simon hit
14 Feature of mesh fabrics
16 The Carolinas, e.g., to the French
17 Debugs computer programs, e.g.
19 Two of racing's Unsers
20 Neighbor of B.C.
21 San ___, Marin County
22 La ___ Tar Pits
23 Bird feeder fill
24 Responds to rashes
31 Like Papa Bear's porridge
32 Collect splinters, so to speak
33 Tuskegee's locale: Abbr.
34 Nutmeg State sch.
35 Ore suffix
36 "What ___" ("Ho-hum")
38 Rap sheet entries, for short
39 Messenger ___
40 Record label owned by Sony
41 Does some mending
45 Cellular construction
46 Overlook
47 One of the Leeward Islands
50 Hesitant sounds
51 Mexicali Mrs.
54 Lines up the sewing
57 Coral creation
58 Blood type historically considered the universal donor
59 Only beardless Disney dwarf
60 Have a knish, say
61 Orbiting telescope launcher

DOWN
1 Florida city, for short
2 Australian gem
3 "Sure, why not?!"
4 Business letter abbr.
5 Return to one's seat?
6 Quarter of Algiers
7 Batter's fig.
8 Ethiopia's Haile ___
9 Glitterati
10 Blah, blah, blah, for short
11 Satirist Mort
12 Skier's turn
13 Gas brand in Canada
15 Prestigious business school
18 Umiak passenger
22 Road, in the Rheinland
24 Speech spot
25 Tiramisu topper
26 Place to rule
27 Business sign abbr.
28 Like Siberian winters
29 Give a lift
30 Long tales
35 What oysters "R" during "R" months
36 Da Vinci or Michelangelo, to Romans
37 Wordsmith's ref.
39 Florenz Ziegfeld offering
40 Set a lofty goal
42 Raw material for Wrigley's, once
43 To a great degree
44 MapQuest offerings
47 Make ___ dash
48 Brussels-based alliance
49 'Vette roof option
51 Islamic sect
52 Amps up
53 On the main
55 ___-Cat (winter vehicle)
56 Doz. eggs, commonly

by Jerry E. Rosman

ACROSS

1 Side of a doorway
5 1928 Oscar winner Jannings
9 ___ and dangerous
14 Actor Morales
15 Western locale called the Biggest Little City in the World
16 Late hotel queen Helmsley
17 Small hotel room specification
20 Modern workout system
21 Fan sound
22 "Hel-I-lp!"
23 Capone and Pacino
25 Sticky stuff
27 1944 thriller with Fred MacMurray and Barbara Stanwyck
36 ___-bitty
37 Falco of "The Sopranos"
38 Ad ___ per aspera (Kansas' motto)
39 Former AT&T rival
40 Princess Diana's family name
42 Suffix with president
43 Eagle's nest
45 Trojan War hero
46 Years, in Latin
47 Baked dessert with lemon filling, maybe
50 Partner of long. in a G.P.S. location
51 Small pouch
52 "___ sells seashells by the seashore" (tongue twister)
54 Bulletin board fastener
58 Oliver's love in "As You Like It"
62 Serious heart surgery
65 Brink
66 Continental money
67 Author Morrison
68 Words to live by
69 TV's warrior princess
70 Former jets to J.F.K.

DOWN

1 Words said in fun
2 Where India is
3 Lion's hair
4 Chronic whiner
5 Before, poetically
6 Cat's plaint
7 1/12 of a foot
8 Graph points
9 Swiss peak
10 Deduces
11 Not stereo
12 Letter attachments: Abbr.
13 When the sun shines
18 Laze about
19 Impulse
24 Ooze
26 Poet Khayyám
27 Probe persistently
28 Stream critter
29 Wombs
30 Like a score of 10 for 10
31 Japanese fighter
32 Go bad, as teeth
33 Singer Turner's autobiography
34 Drug that calms the nerves, slangily
35 New Haven collegian
40 Actress Ward
41 Old flames
44 Start of a daily school recital
46 Opposite of refuses
48 "___, Brute?"
49 Bordering on pornographic
52 Litigant
53 Tortoise's race opponent
55 Peak
56 Word in many a Nancy Drew title
57 "Show Boat" composer Jerome
59 Neighbor of Vietnam
60 "Money ___ everything"
61 Sale tag caution
62 Shopping channel
63 Scarlet
64 Feathered neckwear

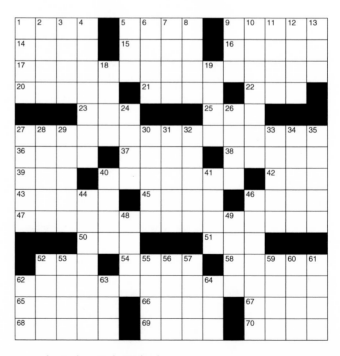

by Andrea Carla Michaels

ACROSS

1 Internet address starter
5 Shoe part
9 Shoe mark
14 Where Donegal Bay is
15 Declare frankly
16 "The Yankee Years" co-writer
17 Word after "ppd." on a sports page
18 Like a 1943 copper penny
19 Desilu co-founder
20 Bitter-tasting vegetable
23 Steps nonchalantly
24 Common commemorative items
28 Mobile's state: Abbr.
29 Garfield's foil
31 The Eiger, for one
32 "Young Indian brave" in a 1960 Johnny Preston #1 hit
36 Even up
37 Arguing loudly
38 Abbr. in a help wanted ad
39 Essen's region
40 "Kid-tested, mother-approved" cereal
41 Least acceptable amount
45 Prefix with tourism
46 Resistance units
47 Unit of RAM, for short
48 Actress Bullock
50 Morphine and codeine, for two
54 Country singer with a hit sitcom
57 Dwelt
60 ___ & Chandon Champagne
61 Village Voice award
62 Baja buddy
63 Munich Mrs.
64 Make out
65 More than a twitch
66 Macy's department
67 S.&L. offerings

DOWN

1 Rosemary and thyme
2 Princess' topper
3 The Dixie Chicks and the Dixie Cups
4 Strong liking
5 "The Human Comedy" novelist William
6 Cameo shapes
7 Actress Loughlin of "90210"
8 Vessel by a basin
9 Less likely to collapse
10 Jazzman Chick
11 Subject of a Keats ode
12 Monk's title
13 Shriner's topper
21 Colombian city
22 Samoan port
25 10-year-old Oscar winner O'Neal
26 Peace Nobelist Root
27 ___ whale
29 Slender woodwinds
30 Consider
32 Landscapers' tools
33 City in New York's Mohawk Valley
34 "Frost/___," 2008 nominee for Best Picture
35 Listerine target
39 Tubular pasta
41 Yawn inducer
42 Melville's obsessed whaler
43 Driving force
44 Deutschland denial
49 Bottom-of-the-barrel stuff
50 Great blue expanse
51 River of Rome
52 Author Jong
53 Is in the market for
55 Like most car radios
56 Oliver Twist's request
57 ___ Cruces, N.M.
58 Handful for a baby sitter
59 Itinerary word

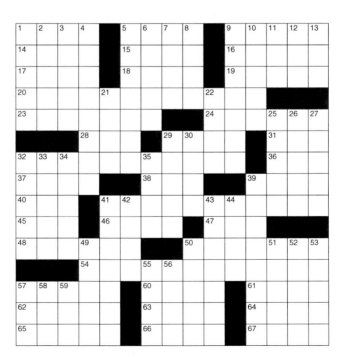

by Allan E. Parrish

ACROSS

1 Frog-dissecting class: Abbr.
5 "Ship of Fools" painter
10 Riot queller
14 Pink, maybe
15 Lawn care brand
16 "Such a pity"
17 Slate, e.g.
18 Where was the Battle of Bunker Hill fought?
20 Makes invalid
22 California Indian tribe: Var.
23 Seminary teaching
24 Drain
25 Cousin of a cat's-eye
29 What animal does a bulldogger throw?
30 Drop __ (moon)
32 Soprano Gluck
33 Get copy right
35 Money
37 In what country are Panama hats made?
41 What is George Eliot's given name?
42 It'll keep the home fires burning
43 Queens's __ Stadium
44 Seed cover
45 Golfer Ballesteros
47 From what animals do we get catgut?
52 Smallest
54 Soft shoe, briefly
55 Part of São Paulo
56 Column style
58 Putting up the greatest affront
59 In what country are Chinese gooseberries produced?
63 Times to call, in some want ads
64 Unoccupied
65 Deejay's interest, typically
66 Port opener?
67 Family dogs, for short
68 Very funny happenings
69 The "I" in M.I.T.: Abbr.

DOWN

1 Challah and baguettes
2 "You are so!" preceder
3 What color is the black box in a commercial jet?
4 Pea, for one
5 Short cuts
6 Bruins' retired "4"
7 What is actor Stewart Granger's family name?
8 For next to nothing, in slang
9 Brick carriers
10 Reddish brown
11 Clay, today
12 "Silent" prez
13 Adult ed. class, often
19 __ Na Na
21 Rio Grande port
24 Recipe verb
26 "M*A*S*H" star
27 Eliot Ness and others
28 Bring home
31 The California gull is the state bird of which state?
34 For what animals are the Canary Islands named?
36 1974 Mocedades hit
37 Not différent
38 __ package
39 Former Voice of America org.
40 Nobody too big or too small, on a sign
41 Fraction of a tick: Abbr.
43 What kind of fruit is an alligator pear?
46 Actor Estevez
48 Cab Calloway phrase
49 How many colleges are in the Big Ten?
50 Ford failures
51 Take care of a neighbor's dog, say
53 Piggy
57 He wrote "If called by a panther, / Don't anther"
58 Nutritional amts.
59 Cowboys' org.
60 Cold war __
61 Site for a site
62 Site for a site

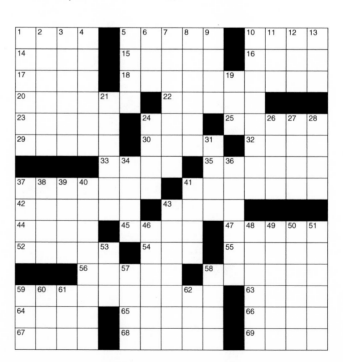

by Ed Stein and Paula Gamache

ACROSS

1 Iditarod vehicle
5 Money for the poor
9 In a stupor
14 Skunk ___ Le Pew
15 Jacob's wife
16 President sworn in on Lincoln's Bible
17 They can be stroked or bruised
18 "Othello" character who says "Who steals my purse steals trash"
19 Bearer of gold, frankincense or 66-Across
20 Speaking with lofty language
23 Cunning
24 "Do ___ others . . ."
25 Riddle
29 Ginger ___ (Canada Dry product)
30 Droop
31 ___ Luthor of "Superman"
32 Withholding nothing
37 Jazz's Fitzgerald
38 October 31 shout
39 Luau garlands
40 What a fresh ad campaign helps combat
45 History segment
46 Auditor's org.
47 Like carrots that crunch
48 Calm
50 Campbell's product
52 Damage
55 Holder of the first-in-the-nation presidential primary
58 "Dancing With the Stars" airer
61 Help in crime
62 Tolkien creatures
63 One getting one-on-one instruction
64 Egg on
65 Sainted fifth-century pope
66 Gift brought to Bethlehem
67 Pb, in chemistry
68 Its cycle is indicated by the starts of 20-, 32-, 40- and 55-Across

DOWN

1 Shoots, as lava
2 Permissible
3 Strong bond
4 Arnaz of "I Love Lucy"
5 Like celestial bodies exhibiting syzygy
6 Pounced (on)
7 Nearsighted Mr. of cartoons
8 What a cobbler works on
9 Santo ___, Caribbean capital
10 Beaded counters
11 Zig's partner
12 Cousin of an ostrich
13 Prosecutors, briefly
21 ___ and void
22 Blue-winged duck
26 3-Down and others
27 Earn
28 x and y, on a graph
29 Jai ___
30 Sean Connery, nationally speaking
32 Airborne signal
33 Like a bone from the elbow to the wrist
34 Bird seen in hieroglyphics
35 Bush 43, to Bush 41
36 Large amount
37 Rams' mates
41 Ancient Assyrian capital
42 Sprouted
43 Blew, as a volcano
44 Notorious B.I.G. releases
49 Key in
50 Buffalo hockey player
51 "Phi, chi, psi" follower
52 Actor Sal of "Exodus"
53 "Star Wars" droid
54 Plant exudation
56 Lug
57 Captain's place
58 Dispenser of 20s
59 Totally accept, as an idea
60 Midpoint: Abbr.

by Dustin Foley

42

ACROSS

1 Pat down
6 Lead character on "Saved by the Bell"
10 On a cruise
14 Neopagan belief
15 Second word of many fairy tales
16 Extremist sect
17 Red Sox Hall-of-Famer Bobby
18 ___ Strauss jeans
19 Spelunker's hangout
20 Valuable discoveries
23 Prevailed
24 Most enlightened
25 Cry while holding a bag
31 Exploding stars
32 Loud chuckles
33 Married mlle.
36 Sch. on the bank of the Rio Grande
37 East ___ (nation since 2002)
38 Billy who sang "We Didn't Start the Fire"
39 Lean-___
40 Ebbed
41 The time it takes mountains to rise
42 Proven to work
44 Cirque du ___
47 Diplomat's bldg.
48 Semi
54 Impulsive
55 Home of Città del Vaticano
56 Less common
58 Letter-routing abbr.
59 Actor McGregor
60 Brilliant display
61 South-of-the-border currency
62 "Well, gosh darn!"
63 Timetables, informally

DOWN

1 Subject line starter on many an e-mail joke
2 Hilarious act
3 Cake decorator
4 Twist-off bottle top
5 Word derived from Japanese for "empty orchestra"
6 Last letter of a pilot's alphabet
7 Imitator
8 Sheltered inlet
9 Sweaters and such
10 Approach aggressively
11 Debonair
12 Dwellers in Middle-earth
13 "This is only ___"
21 ___-cone
22 Narrow inlets
25 Letter-shaped fastener
26 ___-Rooter
27 Currier and ___
28 Riesling wines are produced in its valley
29 Having dams at various locations, as a river
30 Spinoff of "The Mary Tyler Moore Show"
33 What boats may do in an inlet
34 File, Edit or Help
35 "That's something ___"
37 Made to order, as a suit
38 Not just dark
40 Habeas corpus, for one
41 Looks up to
42 Electronic dance genre
43 Teacher's union: Abbr.
44 Amusement park ride feature
45 Hold forth
46 Endures
49 Prime seating spot
50 Untouchable, e.g.
51 "You ___?"
52 Writer ___ Stanley Gardner
53 Go over Time?
57 Football blockers: Abbr.

by Joon Pahk

ACROSS

1 Venetian who explored for England in the 15th century
6 Paints gently
10 Mattress filler during a recession, maybe
14 Last Oldsmobile car
15 Palindromic magazine name
16 "A pity"
17 Tail-less Old World mammal
18 Land of the descendants of 67-Across
19 "Step right up!"
20 An Olympic swimmer needs a big one
23 50+ org.
24 Royal family
28 Less than 1%
31 It may be over a window
35 Tricks
37 Not so common
38 The Greatest
39 Son of, in Arab names
40 Akihito's wife, e.g.
42 Rebelling Turner
43 ___ pooped to pop
44 Shire of "Rocky"
45 Treaty signing
47 Sound practical judgment
50 After 2004, the only way to buy a 14-Across
51 Slander
52 Modern way to put out an album
54 Fateful event for the Titanic
61 Diamond group
64 Runner in Pamplona
65 Like spoken n's
66 It turns a hundred into a thousand
67 Jacob's twin

68 Makes like the Cheshire Cat
69 Element that can precede the starts of 20-, 31-, 47- and 54-Across
70 Where the crew chows down
71 "Poor Richard's Almanack" bit

DOWN

1 Give a ring
2 Baseball's Felipe or Jesus
3 Capital of Switzerland
4 Art form that commonly depicts a swan
5 Puccini opera
6 Group with the 1968 hit "Hush"
7 2006 Emmy winner for "The West Wing"
8 Congressional Black Caucus, e.g.
9 Rest stop sight
10 Echo location
11 Stout, e.g.
12 "Harlem Nocturne" instrument
13 1940s–'50s White House inits.
21 Part of a circle
22 Common companion of a dry throat
25 Astronomical discovery of 1781
26 Grief relief
27 Ready to be typeset
28 Paul Revere and others
29 Big bang
30 Turn a deaf ear to
32 ___ to go
33 Spying against one's own country, say
34 He ran to succeed 13-Down: Abbr.
36 Et ___
41 More, on Mallorca
46 Author Kipling
48 Biblical strongman
49 Part of S.A.S.E.: Abbr.
53 Line dance
55 Hot pair
56 A teaspoonful, maybe
57 Reconstruction and the Roaring Twenties
58 Indian's home
59 Club familiars
60 End of a warning
61 Gun produced by Israel Military Industries
62 La Méditerranée, e.g.
63 Whiz

by Joey Weissbrot

44

ACROSS

1 Best-selling computer game of the 1990s
5 Players in a play
9 Unwanted e-mail
13 Helicopter blade
15 "___ your thirst" (former Sprite slogan)
16 Therefore
17 Myanmar, once
18 Al Capone, for one
20 Mentalist Geller
21 Little devil
23 Breadth
24 Not heeding danger
27 Apartment that's owned, not leased
28 Nick at ___
29 Computer whiz
32 ___ Antonio, Tex.
33 Jobs at Apple
35 Corridors
37 Widespread Internet prank involving a bait-and-switch link to a music video
41 Reason for engine trouble, perhaps
42 Christmas carols
45 ___ and eggs
48 Metal that gave its name to a shade of blue
51 Writer Harte
52 Caribbean vacation spot
54 Mick Jagger or Bruce Springsteen
56 Prayer beads
58 Parisian "yes"
59 Studio that made "Notorious"
60 Packs for bikers and hikers
63 Young pigeon
65 52-Across, e.g.
66 Cry while careering downhill

67 Bulrush, e.g.
68 Fortuneteller
69 Stop or Do Not Pass
70 Almost-failing grades

DOWN

1 Owner of the Springfield Nuclear Power Plant on "The Simpsons"
2 Shout in tag
3 Less forgiving
4 ___ Sawyer
5 Body in a whodunit
6 "The ___ Daba Honeymoon"
7 Fraction of a min.
8 Little fella
9 Fight that might include fisticuffs
10 Prettifies oneself, as in a mirror

11 Order of business at a meeting
12 "When it rains, it pours" salt brand
14 Train travel
19 Be great at
22 Encountered
25 Bandleader Eubanks of "The Jay Leno Show"
26 Learned one
30 "2001" computer
31 Running a temperature, say
34 High-m.p.g. vehicles
36 Hoity-toity sorts
38 Hootchy-___
39 "Spare" part of the body
40 She says "The lady doth protest too much, methinks" in "Hamlet"

43 Problem with pipes
44 Disco lights
45 Joel Chandler ___, creator of Uncle Remus
46 Excite
47 What a bodybuilder builds
49 Undo, as laces
50 Fort Worth sch.
53 Cake maker
55 Smooch
57 Deviations of a ship's course
61 "The Sweetheart of Sigma ___"
62 What's tapped at a beer bust
64 Letters at the end of a proof

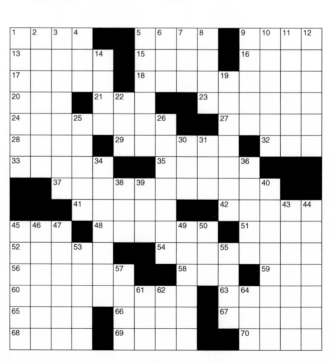

by Natan Last

ACROSS

1 Go 50 in a 30-m.p.h. zone, e.g.
6 Joyful tune
10 Enthusiasm
14 Similar
15 "Are you ___ out?"
16 Utah ski resort
17 1985 Glenn Close/ Jeff Bridges thriller
19 Saint Barthélemy et d'autres
20 German's "Dear me!"
21 Mail service made obsolete by the transcontinental telegraph
23 Fish stew containers
25 Slowly, in music
26 Most Little Leaguers
27 Hay unit
30 Hardly a little angel
32 Simple swimming stroke
37 In a Kinks hit s/he "walked like a woman and talked like a man"
38 Waiters' handouts
39 Mob scene
40 Widening in a highway, maybe
42 Lenin's "What ___ Be Done?"
43 River of Spain
44 Eisenhower and Turner
46 "When You Wish Upon ___"
50 Groveled
53 1970s Robert Young TV role
57 "Gloria in excelsis ___"
58 Farm team
59 What the long Across answers with circles have
61 Go here and there
62 Actress Hathaway

63 "Evil ___" (comics series)
64 Oklahoma city
65 Bat, ball, glove, etc.
66 Number of hills in Roma

DOWN

1 Pat of "Wheel of Fortune"
2 Come in second
3 It's last to be sunk
4 Heart test readout: Abbr.
5 Very much
6 Property claims
7 Four-time Harrison Ford film role
8 Second-level seating
9 Fearsome display at a natural history museum
10 Congo's name before 1997
11 TV's DeGeneres
12 Mushroom producer, for short
13 Rodeo rope
18 Bucks' partners
22 Appeal
24 General Mills brand
27 "Bedtime for ___" (Reagan film)
28 Contents of the Spanish Main
29 8-track alternatives
30 Deli sandwich, for short
31 Kanga's baby
32 Honeybunch
33 Like raisins vis-à-vis grapes
34 Andrei Sakharov in the Soviet era, e.g.
35 Film studio locale
36 W.W. II command
38 World Series org.

41 Where Simón Bolívar was once president
44 The Beatles' "Let ___"
45 Economist John Maynard ___
46 Love, Italian-style
47 The "S" in WASP
48 Rome's ___ Fountain
49 Pimply
50 Tree with catkins
51 Send, as payment
52 "We're off ___ the Wizard . . ."
54 Catch and throw back, as fly balls
55 Burgundy or Bordeaux
56 "The Simpsons" teacher who is called Mrs. K
60 Test for Ph.D. wannabes

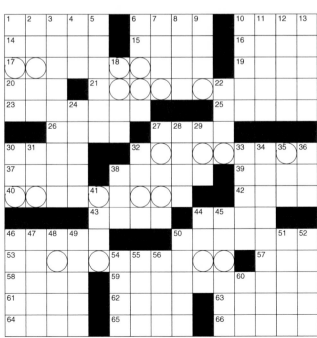

by Barry Boone

ACROSS

1 Booker T.'s bandmates in '60s R&B
4 San Diego Zoo attractions
10 [fizzle]
14 "Can't Get It Out of My Head" grp.
15 "Peter and the Wolf" musician
16 View from Buffalo
17 Have surgery
20 Great time
21 Actress Polo of "Meet the Parents"
22 RR stop
23 ___ David
24 With 37- and 50-Across, privileged
26 Colorful glacier layer
29 Bubble contents
30 Family girl
31 Family girl
34 Dolt
37 See 24-Across
41 Co. acquired by Verizon in 2006
42 Sturdy building material
43 Court figs.
45 D.C. influence wielder
48 Designer's starting point
50 See 24-Across
55 "Keep ___ alive!"
56 Geisha's accessory
57 Diamond legend, with "the"
58 "Bowling for Columbine" documentarian
60 "Gimme!"
64 Mine, in Marseille
65 ___ Palace, French presidential residence
66 Seventh in a series of 24
67 It may be caught in a trap

68 Sure
69 Rogers who was elected twice to the Country Music Hall of Fame

DOWN

1 Sister in "Little Women"
2 Doctrine that de-emphasizes regional interests
3 Barry White's genre
4 Some marine herds
5 Help in a bad way
6 ___'easter
7 "Likewise"
8 One of the 12 tribes of Israel
9 Chest protectors
10 Slammer
11 Bill passed many times on the Hill, formerly

12 It may be taken in court, with "the"
13 Pop/R&B singer ___ Marie
18 Kitty's pickup point
19 Fuzzy fruit
23 "Numb3rs" network
24 They may come in a round
25 Modern locale of ancient Persepolis
27 Accts. payable receipt
28 French bus. firm
32 Winter Minn. hrs.
33 Pleistocene, e.g.
35 Fries, often
36 Began paying attention
38 They may be licked or smacked
39 "Vas ___ Vas" (former derivative Spanish-language game show)

40 Wine: Prefix
44 Geneviève, e.g.: Abbr.
46 Prefix with dextrous
47 Actress Phyllis of "I Was a Teenage Frankenstein"
49 Comrade of Mao
50 Butcher's discards
51 Feminist Wolf who wrote "The Beauty Myth"
52 Bankrupt company in 2002 headlines
53 Curved fastener
54 Milkman of musical fame
58 Talking horse of old TV
59 Mind
61 Hobbyist's purchase
62 Spanish "that"
63 "That's great news!"

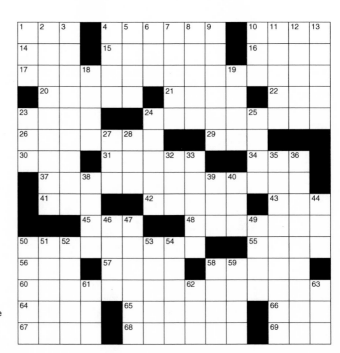

by Michael Vuolo

ACROSS

1 Knights' competition
6 Baby kangaroo
10 Kid around
14 Winfrey who said "I still have my feet on the ground, I just wear better shoes"
15 Feminine suffix
16 Length × width, for a rectangle
17 Brother outlaw in the Wild West
19 Spick-and-span
20 Suffix with pay
21 "___ happy returns"
22 Imbeciles
24 Ones with caws for alarm?
25 Some boxing wins, for short
26 Humiliate
28 Cause for a mistrial
32 Not taut
33 "Tell ___ lies"
34 Prime draft status
35 Googly-eyed Muppet
36 Retail clothing giant . . . or a description of 17- and 54-Across and 10- and 24-Down?
37 Color for baby girls, traditionally
38 L.B.J. son-in-law Charles
39 Things inflated with hot air?
40 Cabalists' plans
41 Mexican beans
43 Makes progress
44 Up to the task
45 19th-century educator Horace
46 Politico Milk of "Milk"
49 Bo : Obama :: ___ : Roosevelt
50 "___ Baba and the 40 Thieves"
53 Jai ___
54 White Sox outfielder nicknamed "Shoeless"
57 Injured
58 Choir voice
59 Discover by chance
60 Home of Iowa State University
61 Back end
62 Midterms and finals

DOWN

1 "___ left his home in Tucson, Arizona" (Beatles lyric)
2 Autobahn auto
3 With 45-Down, home of the Big Dipper
4 Carrier to Copenhagen
5 1994 Jim Carrey film
6 Levi's, e.g.
7 "Time Is ___ Side" (Rolling Stones hit)
8 Opposite of WSW
9 "So you've said"
10 "Me and Bobby McGee" singer, 1971
11 Nabisco cookie
12 Chair or sofa
13 Bowlers that don't bowl
18 "The Gong Show" panelist ___ P. Morgan
23 Hound
24 Longtime New York senator for whom a center is named
25 iPod downloads
26 "It's ___ nothing"
27 Thumper's "deer friend"
28 Give a ___ welcome
29 The "U" in A.C.L.U.
30 Payments to landlords
31 Talks, talks, talks
32 Feudal worker
33 Fibber of old radio
36 Smucker's container
40 Flair
42 U.K. award
43 Black-tie affair
45 See 3-Down
46 "That's rich!"
47 Homecoming attendee, in brief
48 Once in a blue moon
49 Greek cheese
50 Dashiell Hammett hound
51 Tapestry device
52 Places to stay the night
55 Bullring cheer
56 Spherical breakfast cereal

by Randall J. Hartman

48

ACROSS

1 Soft or crunchy snack
5 Like a 52-Across
10 Start of an incantation
14 The "A" in Chester A. Arthur
15 Rudely assertive
16 When repeated, Road Runner's call
17 1908 Cubs player and position
20 How fame comes, sometimes
21 Friars Club event
22 The Braves, on a scoreboard
23 "Pants on fire" person
25 1908 Cubs player and position
33 Chutzpah
34 Put an edge on
35 Hydrotherapy locale
36 "How sweet ___!"
37 Barbers' touch-ups
39 Polish's partner
40 U. of Miami's athletic org.
41 Baseball analyst Hershiser
42 Command to an attack dog
43 1908 Cubs player and position
47 Salt Lake City athletes
48 Ike's W.W. II command
49 "Yes we can" sloganeer
52 2006 Ken Jennings book . . . or the author himself
57 What 17-, 25- and 43-Across were, famously
60 Virginia ___ (noted 1587 birth)
61 The Dapper Don
62 Fountain order
63 Polaris or Sirius
64 Jimmy of the Daily Planet
65 They're splitsville

DOWN

1 "Toodles"
2 Touched down
3 Water-to-wine site
4 Peeling potatoes, stereotypically
5 Mast extensions
6 Bodyguard's asset
7 Only African-American male to win Wimbledon
8 P, on a fraternity house
9 Norse war god
10 Work like paper towels
11 Software test version
12 Vintage autos
13 Date with an M.D.
18 Clear, as a tape
19 The "t" in Nafta
23 Machine with a shuttle
24 Rustic lodgings
25 1946 high-tech wonder
26 Climbing plant with pealike flowers
27 Novelist Jong
28 Homes on wheels, in brief
29 Hot dog topper
30 Humane org. since 1866
31 Black-clad and white-clad Mad adversaries
32 Wonderland cake phrase
37 Logic diagram
38 Flag tossers, for short
39 Bro or sis
41 Of base 8
42 Showing no emotion
44 "Sorry, Wrong ___"
45 Add a star to, say
46 Not leave the house
49 They may be stacked against you
50 Dinghy, e.g.
51 Surrounding glow
52 Nonkosher diner offerings
53 Iditarod terminus
54 Huge-screen format
55 Up to it
56 Hotel room roll-ins
58 Part of Freud's "psychic apparatus"
59 Vote seeker, for short

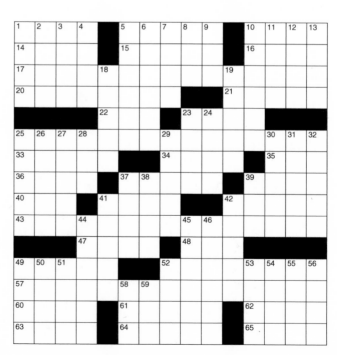

by Ronald J. and Nancy J. Byron

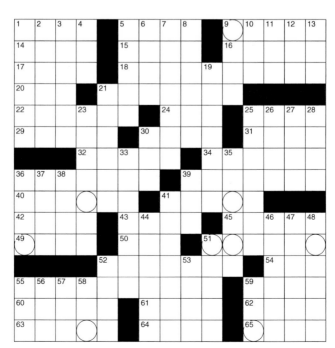

When this puzzle is done, the nine circles will contain the letters A through I. Connect them with a line, in alphabetical order, and you will form an illustration of the puzzle's theme.

ACROSS

1 A Morse "I" consists of two
5 Penultimate fairy tale word
9 Deadly snake
14 "Climb ___ Mountain"
15 Long skirt
16 Break point
17 With 59-Across, A-B-C-A in the illustration
18 Ship in "Pirates of the Caribbean"
20 Stop ___ dime
21 Half of a mountaineering expedition
22 Dressed like a certain keg party attendee
24 Prefix with lateral
25 F-G
29 Ship's christening, e.g.
30 C-D
31 "___ expert, but . . ."
32 Certain California wines
34 Pirating
36 "Top Hat" dancer
39 Does some electrical work on
40 Counterpart of un ángel
41 Santa-tracking org.
42 End in ___
43 A-B
45 Send, as payment
49 E-F-G-H-E
50 Part of U.C.L.A.
51 Brainstorm
52 People in fierce snowball fights
54 Yearbook sect.
55 Ship to the New World
59 See 17-Across
60 Ancient theater
61 Makeup of some little balls

62 Response to a charge
63 Stethoscope users, at times
64 Away from the wind
65 Lava lamps and pet rocks, once

DOWN

1 Bump down but keep on
2 Chekhov play or its antihero
3 "M*A*S*H" procedure
4 Lexicographical abbr.
5 Incorporate, as a YouTube video into a Web site
6 Actor Kilmer and others
7 Horse-race bets on win and place
8 Kitchen gadgets
9 Hook or Cook: Abbr.
10 Tribute with feet
11 Deadly snake
12 1921 play that introduced the word "robot"
13 One of the oceans: Abbr.
19 One who may put you in stitches?
21 Part of a larger picture
23 Poe's "___ Lee"
25 "Don't Go Breaking My Heart" duettist, 1976
26 Mideast V.I.P.
27 Cousin of -trix
28 Old shipbuilding needs
30 Writer Rita ___ Brown
33 Leak on a ship, e.g.
35 Tournament wrap-up
36 Wife of Esau

37 In ___ (as found)
38 Following detective
39 CD-___
41 It may be flared
44 "Yowie, zowie!"
46 "Mississippi ___" (1992 film)
47 Words of resignation
48 Magnetic induction units
51 Livid
52 D– reviews
53 Aachen article
55 ___ sauce
56 Suffix with many fruit names
57 Minus: Abbr.
58 Dress (up)
59 Number on a bottle at the beach

by Daniel A. Finan

ACROSS

1 Part of a Halloween costume
5 Rich soil component
10 Get an ___ effort
14 "Do ___ others as . . ."
15 Not appropriate
16 Duo plus one
17 Mark left from an injury
18 Refuse a request
19 Detained
20 Separate grains from wheat, e.g.
22 Valentine candy message
24 Animated TV character whose best friend is Boots
28 Suffix with access
29 Young dog or seal
30 China's Mao ___-tung
31 ___ Jima
32 Casey of "American Top 40"
34 Main port of Yemen
35 2008 campaign personality
40 Like paintings and some juries
41 As a result
42 Fruity cooler
43 Animal pouch
46 Plane takeoff guess: Abbr.
47 Chicken ___ king
50 Norman Rockwell painting subject of W.W. II
54 Fix permanently, as an interest rate
55 Helmet from W.W. I or W.W. II
56 "Beauty ___ the eye . . ."
58 Semiconductor giant
60 Idiot
61 Tenth: Prefix
62 Hospital attendant
63 Kuwaiti leader
64 Business V.I.P.
65 Velocity
66 Say "No, I didn't"

DOWN

1 High-priority item
2 Katie Couric, for one
3 Like the night sky
4 Seoul's home
5 Top-secret
6 Italian article
7 Answer that's between yes and no
8 Coming immediately after, as on TV
9 Leaves in a huff, with "out"
10 Prefix with -centric
11 Something for nothing, as what a hitchhiker seeks
12 OPEC product
13 Fishing pole
21 March 17 honoree, for short
23 ___ de France
25 Sword of sport
26 Fancy pitcher
27 Politico ___ Paul
32 Beer blast centerpiece
33 Measure of a car's 65-Across: Abbr.
34 Lincoln, informally
35 Cousin of karate
36 Minimum pizza order
37 Lusty look
38 Like the Beatles' White Album
39 The year 1406
40 Part of a guffaw
43 1/60 of a min.
44 Diet doctor
45 "Don't let it get you down!"
47 Comfortable (with)
48 Go right at it, as work
49 Vein's counterpart
51 Kind of column, in architecture
52 ___ nous (between us)
53 Kaput
56 Suffix with chlor-
57 It sells in advertising, they say
59 180° from WNW

by Joe Krozel

51

ACROSS

1 They put the frosting on the cake
6 Grant's is in New York
10 ___ as a post
14 Pacific archipelago nation
15 "Young Frankenstein" role
16 Golden State sch.
17 Fix the hair just so, say
18 Bind with a band
19 Actress Singer of "Footloose"
20 ___ as an arrow
22 Jug capacity
24 ___ as a pin
25 ___ as a fox
26 ___ as an ox
29 Outlaw Barrow
30 "Bingo!"
31 Newton's Black Panther Party co-founder
33 Barbecue remnants
37 ___ as an owl
39 Command to a dog
41 ___ as a dog
42 Some chips, maybe
44 Less loony
46 4 on a telephone
47 Bottom dog
49 Some chips
51 Theme of this puzzle
54 Eric who played 2003's Hulk
55 Like, with "with"
56 ___ as an eel
60 Chowderheads
61 Sparkling wine locale
63 Indoor trees may grow in them
64 Words after "woe"
65 One end of a hammer

66 ___ as a judge
67 ___ as a doornail
68 ___ as a diamond
69 The way things are going

DOWN

1 AOL and others
2 Auto denter in a supermarket parking lot
3 Leader in a robe
4 Italian cheese
5 Latin for 37-Across
6 ___ as a drum
7 Doing the job
8 Apartment bldg. V.I.P.
9 The Joker in Batman movies, e.g.
10 Tedium
11 Gastroenteritis cause, maybe
12 Baseball All-Star every year from 1955 to 1975
13 Impulsive indulgence
21 Light green plums
23 Lawrence Welk's "one"/"two" connector
25 ___ as a whistle
26 Fellers in the woods?
27 ___ as a rail
28 Literally, "scraped"
29 ___ as a bell
32 Cathedral recesses
34 ___ as a kite
35 Repetitive reply
36 Nordic runners
38 Overshadowed
40 Alaskan peninsula where Seward is located

43 Nut for caffeine?
45 Told to in order to get an opinion
48 Angelic figure
50 Prisoner's opposite
51 ___ as a rock
52 Busy
53 Volcanic buildup
54 ___ as a bat
56 Suffix with pun
57 Kathryn of "Law & Order: Criminal Intent"
58 It means nothing to Sarkozy
59 Area within a picket fence, say
62 Pirate's realm

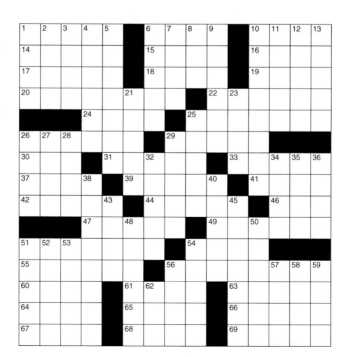

by Matt Ginsberg

52

ACROSS

1 *Start of a 38-Across
5 "The Good Earth" heroine
9 So last year
14 ___ about
15 *Small part of a spork
16 Recyclable item
17 Prayer wheel user
18 *Musical quality
19 Strike down
20 Cockpit announcements, briefly
21 Millstone
22 *Made tracks
23 Strength
25 Cord unit
27 Good name for an investment adviser?
29 Permanently attached, in zoology
32 Early MP3-sharing Web site
35 *Teed off
37 Up-to-date
38 Hint to the word ladder in the answers to the starred clues
43 ". . . and that's final!"
44 *Put into piles
45 Canal site, maybe
47 Showing irritation
52 Last in a series
53 Toxic pollutant, for short
55 Sweet, in Italy
56 *Locale in a western
59 Many Christmas ornaments
62 Holly
63 Crossword maker or editor, at times
64 *It may precede a stroke
65 Rat Pack nickname

66 Dirección sailed by Columbus
67 *Ax
68 Change components, often
69 Dag Hammarskjöld, for one
70 Some cameras, for short
71 *End of a 38-Across

DOWN

1 At minimum
2 How baseball games rarely end
3 Kind of land
4 Undoes
5 Camp Swampy dog
6 Symbol of courage
7 Undo
8 "Kinsey" star, 2004

9 Orkin victim
10 Survivalist's stockpile
11 Full of energy
12 "The Way of Perfection" writer
13 Word after red or dead
24 Solomon's asset
26 In profusion
28 Pseudo-cultured
30 Stockpile
31 Muff one
33 Like some men's hair
34 Nasdaq buy: Abbr.
36 Wynn and Harris
38 Quick drive
39 Tried out at an Air Force base
40 Theater for niche audiences

41 Medical research org.
42 Doo-___
46 Shows scorn
48 Lacking
49 "Fighting" athletes
50 Part of an act, perhaps
51 Simple sugar
54 Range setting
57 On Soc. Sec., say
58 Trap, in a way
60 Winter exclamation
61 Goes with
63 Orgs. with "Inc." in their names

by Barry C. Silk

ACROSS

1 In ___ land (daydreaming)
5 Boeing products
9 Path around the earth
14 Greek vowels
15 Elvis Presley's middle name
16 Battery brand
17 Succumbing to second thoughts
20 Beatnik's "Got it!"
21 "Salut!," in Scandinavia
22 Concorde, in brief
23 Performed prior to the main act
25 What it takes to tango
26 "That's all ___ wrote"
27 Neither's partner
28 Billiard sticks
31 One still in the game, in poker
33 Submit, as homework
35 Low digits
36 Succumbing to second thoughts
40 Mare's newborn
41 Colbert ___ (Comedy Central show audience)
42 Blunders
45 978-0060935443, for Roget's Thesaurus
46 U.K. record label
49 Genetic material
50 Hunky-dory
52 Sailor
54 ___ and downs
55 How Santa dresses, mostly
58 Anatomical passages
59 Succumbing to second thoughts

62 Start of the Spanish calendar
63 Biblical captain for 40 days and 40 nights
64 Golden ___ (senior citizen)
65 Two-door or four-door car
66 Friend in war
67 Unfreeze

DOWN

1 Veterans' group, informally
2 Returning to the previous speed, in music
3 Agitated state
4 Actor/brother Sean or Mackenzie
5 Dutch painter Steen
6 Energy units
7 Tick-___
8 High-hatter
9 Fewer than 100 shares
10 Fight adjudicator, for short
11 "Gesundheit!"
12 Arctic covering
13 Walks unsteadily
18 Drug used to treat poisoning
19 Statutes
24 Easy two-pointer in basketball
29 Genesis garden
30 Mount ___, where the Commandments were given to Moses
32 Loads
33 Largest city on the island of Hawaii
34 Tiny criticisms
36 Dixie bread

37 Pestered
38 Writing points
39 Entered
40 Old schoolmasters' sticks
43 Ruin, as one's parade
44 Any one of the Top 40
46 Come out
47 ___ Comics, home of Spider-Man and the Fantastic Four
48 Add with a caret, e.g.
51 Swedish coin
53 Starting group of athletes
56 Certain alkene
57 Order to the person holding the deck of cards
60 Author Levin
61 Not camera-ready?

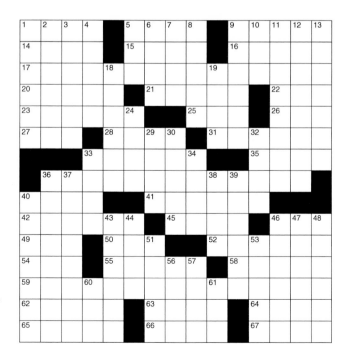

by Mark Milhet

54

ACROSS

1 Cheney's successor as vice president
6 Prize in the ad biz
10 ___ irregular basis
14 Hersey's "A Bell for ___"
15 Prefix with nautical
16 Count (on)
17 Decide against reorganizing the pet store?
20 Mediterranean tree
21 Geog. or geol.
22 Stagehands' items
23 Picked out of a lineup
25 Ankle-related
28 Announcement from a cockpit, for short
30 Doughnut-shaped
32 Very chocolaty, say
33 Finish shooting a movie
34 Bathroom fixture
36 Break in the day
37 Cousin of beige
38 Conversation-filled places in a restaurant?
42 Oscar winner Winslet
43 ___ Aviv, Israel
44 Evil computer in "2001"
45 Mother of Horus
46 Sign of the future
48 Come up again and again
52 Computer connection choice
53 Massless particle
55 A MS. might come back in it
56 Make a connection with
58 "Au Revoir, ___ Enfants"
60 Pre-___ (undergrad study)
61 What chicks have?

65 "Deutschland ___ Alles"
66 "Windows to the soul"
67 Amazingly coincidental
68 Zero
69 Certain conifers
70 "The Devil Wears ___"

DOWN

1 Mismatch
2 Musical whose opening song is "All the Dearly Beloved"
3 What a flashing red light may indicate
4 Suffix with differ
5 Jules et Jim, par exemple
6 Expensive eggs
7 Washington and ___ University
8 Certain savings plan, for short
9 Sound from a 38-Down
10 Very small pasta
11 Pacific Northwest tribe
12 Baseball V.I.P.'s
13 Comedian Louis
18 When Canada celebrates Thanksgiving: Abbr.
19 Web address
24 Airheads
26 Hair curl
27 Nonsense singing
29 Clerk on "The Simpsons"
31 Since, slangily
33 "Citizen Kane" director
35 Nestlé candy

38 Low-pitched instrument
39 Availed oneself of
40 Whom Marlin sought in a 2003 film
41 Tavern
42 Young goat
47 Amazingly enough
49 Cell phone feature, often
50 Computer handle
51 Sudan/Saudi Arabia separator
53 Sch. group
54 Largest U.S. labor union: Abbr.
57 Old Testament book
59 Dance lesson
61 Enjoyment
62 Hide the gray, say
63 Many's opposite
64 "How Stella Got ___ Groove Back"

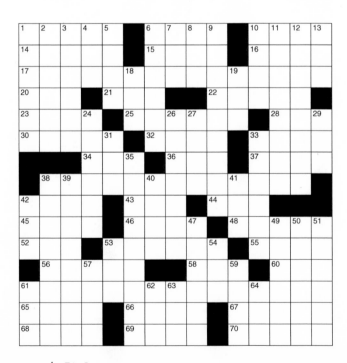

by Trip Payne

ACROSS

1 No. crunchers
5 Haute cuisine it's not
9 Places for links
14 Rope material
15 Audiophile's concern
16 Of service
17 307 for Wyoming and 907 for Alaska
19 El Líder de Argentina
20 Not paying immediately at the bar
22 100 or so, e.g.: Abbr.
23 Use a prie-dieu
24 Adoptee in Genesis
26 2002 Adam Sandler title role
29 Building beams
30 Through the uprights
31 Hams it up
34 "Whew!"
35 Google search need . . . or a hint to the ends of 20- and 49-Across and 11- and 28-Down
38 Satisfied sound
39 Like drinks with umbrellas
41 Fraternal letters
42 Sax type
43 "A diamond is forever" sloganeer
46 Lower oneself
47 Deduces, with "out"
48 Pewter component
49 Go ballistic
54 "Socrate" composer Erik
56 1978 Cheech & Chong movie
57 "It's the end of __"
58 "Holy __!"
59 Line of rotation
60 Less typical
61 Morel morsel
62 Duma dissent

DOWN

1 Burn on the grill
2 Machu Picchu's land
3 "You said it!"
4 Punished with a wooden spoon, say
5 Like Cheech & Chong, typically
6 41-Across meeting places
7 Center Shaq
8 Annoying type
9 China's place
10 Beehive State native
11 Apartment building feature
12 Dental hygienist's advice
13 In the mail
18 Cannes film
21 __ Alert (abduction bulletin)
25 Majorca Mrs.
26 Those in charge: Abbr.
27 Crowd sound
28 Road sign warning
29 1961 Literature Nobelist Andric
31 Harry Potter's pet Hedwig, e.g.
32 Hammer-wielding god
33 "__ All That" (Freddie Prinze Jr. film)
35 Cordelia's father
36 Low-budget prefix
37 Yevtushenko's "Babi __"
40 Louvre pyramid architect
41 Reception toast giver
43 Easily managed
44 Penn, to Pennsylvania
45 Uncle __ rice
46 Paul Anka #1 hit
47 Greyhound stop
48 Autocrat until 1917
50 Bottom lines
51 Classic Manhattan theater
52 Dust Bowl migrant
53 For fear that
55 Ill temper

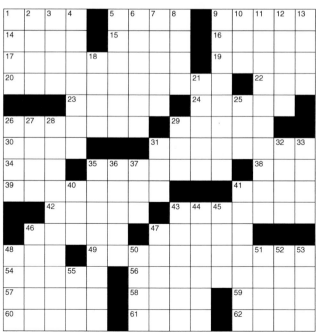

by Michael Callaway Barnhart

ACROSS

1 Africa's ___ Victoria
5 Rope material
9 Letter after beta
14 ___ of March
15 Theater award
16 Bird-related
17 1971 Tom Jones hit
19 Appealingly piquant
20 Photocopier cartridge contents
21 Weeper of Greek myth
23 Perfumery emanations
25 Hot sauce brand
30 1972 Carly Simon hit
33 Items on which baseball insignia appear
37 Opposite of post-
38 Seasons or deices
39 Have ___ (be connected)
40 Bergen dummy Mortimer
43 Words of understanding
44 Windshield flip-down
46 Geese formation shape
47 Finishing 11th out of 11, e.g.
48 1966 Monkees hit
52 Photographers, informally
53 Parish leader
58 ___ chip, which might be topped with 19-Across 27-Down dip
61 Still kicking
62 ___ the Hutt of "Star Wars"
66 1962 Crystals hit
68 Martian or Venusian
69 ___ May Clampett of "The Beverly Hillbillies"
70 Suffix with concession
71 Poet Stephen Vincent ___
72 Gin flavoring
73 London art gallery

DOWN

1 Rosters
2 Kind of committee
3 New Hampshire college town
4 Krupp Works city
5 Christmas or Thanksgiving: Abbr.
6 Abba of Israel
7 Longish skirt
8 Mescaline-yielding cactus
9 Garden pavilions
10 N.Y.C.'s Park or Lex
11 Prefix with place or print
12 Yoga class surface
13 "___ takers?"
18 Pseudo-stylish
22 English majors' degs.
24 Absorbs, with "up"
26 Be of use
27 Tex-Mex preparation
28 Uses as a reference
29 Beginning stage
31 Makeshift vote receptacle
32 Superman portrayer Christopher
33 Be nitpicky
34 Japanese cartoon art
35 Native of the Leaning Tower city
36 Nose-in-the-air sorts
41 Minister's nickname
42 Animal that may be caught in the headlights
45 Carpet leftover
49 Meadow
50 Rainfall units
51 Derrière
54 Golf shoe gripper
55 Fibula's neighbor
56 Plain to see
57 C.S.A. general
59 Satan's domain
60 Norway's capital
62 Sharp left or right, in the ring
63 Ginger ___
64 Bargain basement container
65 Quilting party
67 Sailor's assent

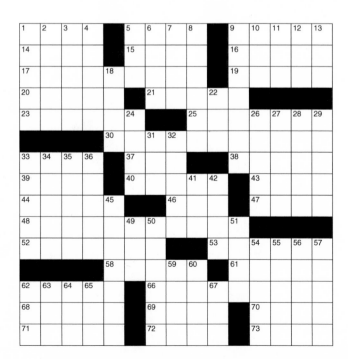

by Fred Piscop

ACROSS

1 Get some sun
4 Blow one's stack
9 Kid-lit pachyderm
14 Naked ___ jaybird
15 Sine, cosine or tangent
16 Tourist mecca off the coast of Venezuela
17 "Beat swords into plowshares"
20 Way off
21 Parasol's offering
22 Cathedral area
23 Grazed, say
25 Silver of the silver screen
27 "Ignore the red, white and blue"
35 Marx Brothers-like
36 Meat favored by Sarah Palin
37 With 44-Across, a traditional Catholic prayer
39 Ring decisions, for short
40 Chuck who sang "Maybellene"
41 Petty quarrel
42 Moray, for one
43 "Peachy keen!"
44 See 37-Across
45 "Oust from practice, then interrogate"
48 Take steps
49 The "A" in MoMA
50 Shi'ite leader
53 Typical John Wayne film
57 Stir up
61 "Scatter while fleeing"
64 Neptune's realm
65 Word before city or tube
66 Etiquette guru Vanderbilt
67 Smallest possible
68 Has to have
69 Masseur's place

DOWN

1 Bit of verbal trumpeting
2 "A likely story"
3 Shuttle org.
4 Pull a boner
5 Any of several Egyptian kings
6 Six-sided state
7 ___ colada
8 Rocker Rundgren
9 Ovine sound
10 Giorgio of fashion
11 Fist ___ (modern greeting)
12 Lincoln and others
13 Like proverbial hen's teeth
18 A Musketeer
19 Rejection of church dogma
24 Behavioral quirk
26 Rich rock
27 Palm fruit
28 Put one's John Hancock on
29 Vodka brand, informally
30 Makeup mishap
31 Main artery
32 Mental midget
33 Blue Grotto's isle
34 To no ___
38 List-ending abbr.
40 Bang, as a drum
41 "No Exit" dramatist
43 "30 Rock" network
44 Dugout V.I.P.: Abbr.
46 Rio dances
47 Moved like a hummingbird
50 Miley Cyrus, to teens
51 Owls' prey
52 Where pirates go
54 Score after deuce
55 Mute, with "down"
56 Feminine suffix
58 Portfolio holdings, briefly
59 Sugar unit
60 One-named New Age singer
62 Tiny colonist
63 Four-baggers: Abbr.

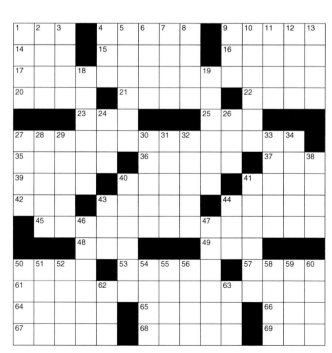

by Wayne and P. K. King

58

ACROSS

1 Windy City team
5 "Me, me, me" sort
9 Like a teddy bear
14 Summer Games org.
15 Radiate
16 Steinbeck migrants
17 Certain mortgage, briefly
18 All over
19 Successfully defend
20 Spicy bar fare
23 Turns, in a way
24 It may have orchids or plumerias
25 Ceremonial utterance
28 Yellow
32 Author Ferber
36 Kiltie's turndown
37 Wipe out
38 Cape Cod town
40 Baseball bigwigs, for short
42 Largish combo
43 Lacking melanin
45 Where It.'s at
47 "Dear" ones
48 Game to 11 points
51 Milk source
52 Crew leader
53 Place for pampering
58 Easy preparation instruction . . . or a hint to the starts of 20-, 28- and 48-Across
61 Big cheese
64 Form of silica
65 Group of thousands, maybe
66 Muscat native
67 Comstock's find
68 Scoreboard tally
69 One, for one
70 Sail support
71 2004 Brad Pitt film

DOWN

1 Cuts back
2 Finish off
3 Super, in showbiz
4 "Futurama" genre
5 Buys and sells
6 "___ expert, but . . ."
7 Op-ed's offering
8 Freely
9 Pardoned
10 Luau strings
11 Mail aid
12 Zuider ___
13 Fashion monogram
21 Tide competitor
22 Frau's "forget it"
25 Certain Oriental rug maker
26 Ward off
27 "Golden Boy" playwright
29 Internet annoyance
30 Red Sea land
31 They may clash
32 Les ___-Unis
33 1964 Tony Randall title role
34 Having a rough knotted surface
35 Seed covering
39 18 inches, give or take
41 Radiation source
44 Siouan speakers
46 "Batman" villain, with "the"
49 Sings the praises of
50 Go back and forth in the woods?
54 America's Cup entrant
55 Flight part
56 Green topping
57 Too-too
58 Mitchell who wrote and sang "Chelsea Morning"
59 Per unit
60 Jean Arp's movement
61 Signal at Christie's
62 "___ losing it?"
63 Avocation, slangily

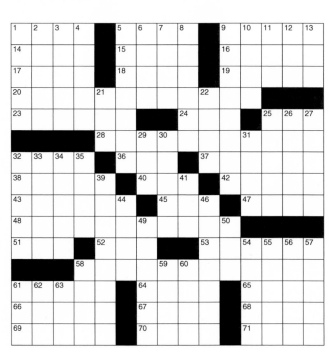

by Nancy Kavanaugh

ACROSS

1 "___ or charge?"
5 Winger or Messing
10 Suffix with song or slug
14 Rights org.
15 Go inside
16 Parisian girlfriend
17 Graham cracker pie shell
19 Binges
20 Poster paints
21 President who followed Harry
23 AOL or MSN: Abbr.
24 18-wheeler
25 Exhausted
26 Spider or worm
31 Delights in
34 Molecule part
35 Tint
36 Bog material
37 Freezer cubes
38 Spreadsheet contents
39 Bond creator Fleming
40 Lois of the Daily Planet
42 Pan-fries
44 Lending crisis
47 ___ I.R.A. (savings plan for old age)
48 Tippler
49 Engineering sch. in Troy, N.Y.
52 Fruit for a monkey
55 Common burger topper
57 All in a twitter
58 Cajun seafood dish
60 Make over
61 Friend of Fran and Ollie
62 At the peak of
63 Garden of ___
64 Exorbitant
65 "Hey, you!"

DOWN

1 Prickly plants
2 Real estate units
3 Batter's dry spell
4 Camel feature
5 Criticizes openly
6 Infuriate
7 A/C measures
8 Hi-___ monitor
9 Style of the 1920s and '30s
10 Tex-Mex treat
11 Online 'zine
12 Sound of relief
13 Try out
18 Fruit on a bush
22 Toasty
25 Computer memory measure
26 Foldaway bed
27 Harness racer
28 One of the five W's
29 Minstrel's instrument
30 Votes opposite the nays
31 The "Odyssey" or "Beowulf"
32 Close by
33 Tarzan's love
37 Ruler division
38 "Well, that's obvious!"
40 Cowardly resident of Oz
41 Blitzes
42 Year-round Alp topper
43 Cast member
45 Fire-breathing beast
46 Functional
49 Mob scenes
50 Collared pullovers
51 Bumbling
52 Like Mother Hubbard's cupboard
53 Ripened
54 Bump on a branch
55 Autumn tool
56 Twice-a-month tide
59 Dirt road feature

by Billie Truitt

60

ACROSS

1 Industry honcho
5 "Do the ___!"
9 Suffix with beer or fun
13 Move, in Realtor lingo
14 XM ___
15 In the old days
16 Lunchbox dessert item
17 Jump for joy
18 "The Good Earth" heroine
19 Tom Collins or Rob Roy
21 Turkic people
23 Grass bought in rolls
24 End of an exhaust system
26 Beehive State athlete
29 Guitar pioneer Paul
31 Paddler's target
32 Unrealistic idea
35 Hold back, as a news story
39 Salon sound
40 In a foxy fashion
42 "Uh-uh"
43 Regatta entry
45 1992 U.S. Olympic hoopsters, with "the"
47 Peseta's replacement
49 La-la lead-in
50 ___-mo
51 Basketball or baseball
55 Ike's monogram
57 Tangle in a net: Var.
58 Fighting rooster
63 Hair removal brand
64 Take forcibly, old-style
66 Tom Wolfe novel "___ in Full"
67 Bigger than mega-
68 Elizabeth of cosmetics
69 After-beach wear
70 Supersecure airline
71 Name on toy fuel trucks
72 Two caplets, say

DOWN

1 Swamp menace, for short
2 Total loser
3 Guinness or Waugh
4 Corner pieces, in chess
5 Ankle-length dress
6 X-rated
7 Up to, in ads
8 Real babe
9 Evidence washed away by the tide
10 China's Zhou ___
11 Bluff formed by a fault
12 In need of a rubdown
14 Blogger's audience
20 Ratted (on)
22 "Sad to say . . ."
25 Decorative band
26 "___-daisy!"
27 Fey of "30 Rock"
28 Huge in scope
30 Only now and then
33 Short-lived
34 Firth of Clyde town
36 The "ten" in "hang ten"
37 Stone for many Libras
38 Nautilus skipper
41 Landscaper's crew
44 Harbor workhorses
46 Showed up in time for
48 Gung-ho
51 Trace of color
52 Messages that may contain emoticons
53 Old computer
54 "Zounds!"
56 Paperless birthday greeting
59 Birds, collectively
60 1847 Melville work
61 Some urban rides
62 "Trick" body part
65 Before, to a bard

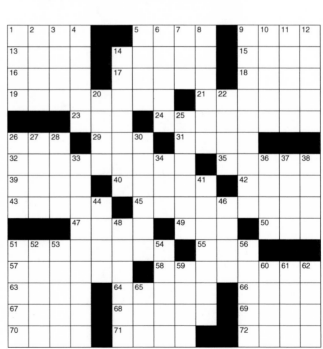

by Damon J. Gulczynski

ACROSS

1 Actor Assante
7 Imprison
12 Mil. rank
15 Oregonian
16 Frost lines
17 Netscape acquirer
18 Entrance requirement, maybe
20 Meter-candle
21 Barack Obama, 2005–08, e.g.
23 Part of Santa's bagful
24 ___ Enterprise
25 1950s White House resident
27 Rookie's superstition
32 Skier's wish
34 Archaeological find
35 "Just kidding!"
36 Texas city . . . and a hint to the starts of 21-, 27-, 45- and 56-Across
42 ___-wop
43 Bum ___
44 To be, to Brutus
45 Subsidiary member of a firm
51 Blockage remover
52 Actress ___ Ling of "The Crow"
53 Fool
56 Some restaurant and pharmacy lures
62 Feel awful
63 French Academy's 40 members
64 Classic British two-seaters
65 Vapid
66 Ogle
67 Like Dvorák's "Serenade for Strings"
68 Philosopher Kierkegaard
69 Gauge

DOWN

1 Toward the stern
2 Not an original
3 "Ahoy, ___!"
4 Company with the stock symbol CAR
5 Belg. neighbor
6 Solicit, as business
7 Still
8 Subway Series participant
9 "Desperate Housewives" role
10 Part of PTA: Abbr.
11 Bring back to domestication
12 Gold-colored horses
13 Multipurpose, somehow
14 160, to Caesar
19 Place for a gauge, informally
22 Persian for "crown"
26 Bus. card info
27 Tijuana tanner
28 Pooh pal
29 High school dept.
30 Little bit
31 Messenger ___
32 Half-salute
33 Only you
37 Make a clanger
38 Clothing retailer since 1969
39 Air monitor, for short
40 Shirt to wear with shorts
41 Mideast land: Abbr.
42 CD players
46 Days ___
47 Ear inflammation
48 Ones who drive people home?
49 Australian island: Abbr.
50 San ___, Christmas figure in Italy
53 Entrap
54 World record?
55 Attention getters
57 [Gasp!]
58 Tail end
59 Sup
60 Tram loads
61 Shoshone speakers
62 Ennemi's opposite

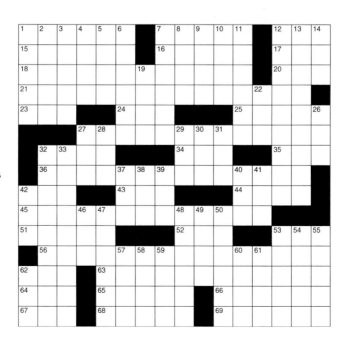

by Ashish Vengsarkar

ACROSS

1 Home (in on)
5 Arrow shooters
9 Hunk
13 Lumberjacks' tools
14 Margarine
15 Uneaten part of an apple
16 Small milk carton capacity
17 Ken of "thirtysomething"
18 Eager
19 1989 Sally Field/ Dolly Parton/Shirley MacLaine movie
22 Hold up
23 Hunk
24 Foresail
27 "Here's to you!" and others
29 Old Pontiac
32 Electrical device for foreign travelers
34 "Git!"
35 2000 Martin Lawrence movie
39 Swamps
40 Cork
41 Novelist Tan
42 Seeks blindly
45 ___ Lanka
46 With 51-Down, John Ashcroft's predecessor as attorney general
48 Legal matter
50 1992 Alec Baldwin/Meg Ryan film
56 Not imaginary
57 Jai ___
58 "To Live and Die ___"
59 The "A" in A.D.
60 Lunkhead
61 Santa's landing place
62 Part of M.V.P.

63 Pitch
64 Thing hidden in each of the movie names in this puzzle

DOWN

1 Microwaves
2 Stage direction after an actor's last line
3 Philosopher Descartes
4 Blender maker
5 Classic John Lee Hooker song of 1962
6 Earthenware pot
7 Puts on a scale
8 One of Shakespeare's begins "Shall I compare thee to a summer's day?"
9 Milan's La ___
10 Some trophies

11 Diva's number
12 They have headboards and footboards
20 Game with a $100 million prize, maybe
21 Meditation syllables
24 "Star Wars" villain ___ the Hutt
25 "Knock it off" or "get it on," e.g.
26 Hip-hop wear
28 One of an octopus's octet
30 Police stunner
31 Onetime "S.N.L." player Cheri
33 Evenings, briefly
34 Soak (up)
36 Egyptian cobra
37 Shots taken by some athletes

38 Old Testament prophet
42 Bearded beast
43 Edit
44 Verdi hero married to Desdemona
47 Apportion
49 Mini or tutu
50 Nanny's vehicle
51 See 46-Across
52 New Mexico resort
53 "Are you ___ out?"
54 Gin flavoring
55 Not out

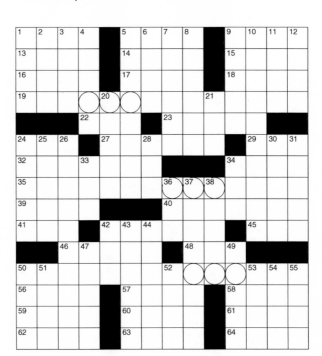

by Peter A. Collins

ACROSS

1 With 66-Across, first in a series of five TV personalities (1954–57)
6 With 65-Across, second in a series of five TV personalities (1957–62)
10 "Think" sloganeer
13 Dropped flies and bad throws, in baseball
15 Sheltered from the wind
16 Teachers' org.
17 Fifth in a series of five TV personalities (starting June 1, 2009)
19 With 22-Across, fourth in a series of five TV personalities (1992–2009)
20 Football six-pointers, for short
21 Since way back when
22 See 19-Across
23 Teacher's teaching
24 Norse race of gods
25 "La Bohème" heroine
28 Closest friends
30 Free from worry
33 Two halved
34 & 35 Third in a series of five TV personalities (1962–92)
40 Scot's cap
42 French actress Catherine
43 Despise
48 Minor hang-up
49 Unaccompanied performances
50 Taunt
53 Desk job at 58 & 59-Across?
54 Decrease
55 Con's opposite
58 & 59 TV home for this puzzle's five featured TV personalities
61 Suffix with ball
62 Opening stake

63 Prompt
64 Telephone book info: Abbr.
65 See 6-Across
66 See 1-Across

DOWN

1 Religious offshoot
2 Trampled
3 Sea eagles
4 U.S. broadcaster overseas
5 Bert's "Sesame Street" pal
6 Tech talk, e.g.
7 Not consistent with, as a way of thinking
8 Middling grades
9 Author Follett
10 How quips are delivered
11 Close-fitting cap
12 City hall leaders
14 Daughters' counterparts

18 Bandleader Count ___
22 Good place to have a cow?
23 Property claim
24 "He doesn't have ___ bone in his body"
25 Not minor: Abbr.
26 "How was ___ know?"
27 Speed limit abbr.
29 Early film director Thomas H. ___
31 "Nay" sayers
32 Shade of blue
36 Observe the Sabbath
37 The Sabbath, to Christians: Abbr.
38 Eggs in a lab
39 Less than zero: Abbr.
41 Purplish tint
42 Clear of defects, as software
43 Actor Kutcher
44 [Sob!]

45 Twins Mary-Kate and Ashley
46 Bon ___ (clever remark)
47 Neater
51 Bounce back, as sound
52 Insurance provider since 1850
54 Jaffe or Barrett
55 Grammy-winning Collins
56 All roads lead to this, they say
57 Wilson of "Zoolander"
59 Strike lightly
60 Letters on a Cardinals cap

by John Farmer

66

ACROSS

1 Recorder input: Abbr.
4 "Beloved" author Morrison
8 Run through
14 All ___ day's work
15 "What ___ for Love" ("A Chorus Line" song)
16 Setting for C. S. Lewis's "The Lion, the Witch and the Wardrobe"
17 Mountain shelter
19 Travels like a flying squirrel
20 Parched
21 Time off, to a sailor
23 Optometrist's concern
25 Poet Khayyám
26 Lawman Wyatt
28 Disfigure
29 Sound from a terrier
32 Endangered feline
36 Name before Cool or Camel
37 Office setting?
38 "Holy Toledo!"
39 Spring time: Abbr.
40 Supped
41 "Arabesque" actress, 1966
46 Lad
47 Rainbow component
48 Surmounting
49 Elusive Himalayan creature
50 99 and 86, on "Get Smart"
54 Highway posting
59 Like Hotspur's horse in "King Henry IV, Part I"
60 Where Hudson Bay is
61 Where rupees are spent
63 The Carnegie of Carnegie Mellon University
64 Dorothy ___ of "The Wizard of Oz"
65 Apostrophized preposition
66 Abbr. preceding multiple surnames
67 Places for play things?
68 TV staple for over 30 years (and a hint to 17-, 21-, 32-, 41-, 54- and 61-Across)

DOWN

1 "Divine" showbiz nickname
2 One way to sing
3 Egypt's capital
4 Spanish uncle
5 "Most likely . . ."
6 Near
7 Prefix with logical
8 Former heavyweight champion Johansson
9 Duck type
10 Snoop
11 Shave ___ haircut
12 Schreiber of the "Scream" films
13 Leisure
18 Cartoon skunk Pepé ___
22 Birthplace of Elie Wiesel
24 Suffix with different
27 Italian archaeological locale
29 Cracked open
30 Lariat
31 Bit of green in a floral display
32 Try
33 Alliance since '49
34 Do as told
35 Cry of disbelief
41 Cat or dog, especially in the spring
42 Jesse James and gang
43 Cocked
44 What an andiron holds
45 Wagner composition
49 Sentence units
51 They're verboten
52 Spoken for
53 Complicated situation
54 Hustle
55 Glazier's sheet
56 Extremities
57 In-box fill: Abbr.
58 "Dies ___" (hymn)
62 "___ Liaisons Dangereuses"

by Patrick Blindauer

ACROSS

1 Like some fevers
9 Title role for Ben Kingsley
15 Tiny, as a town
16 It's north of the Strait of Gibraltar
17 Some long flights
18 Teeming, as with bees
19 Fabric amts.
20 Letter sign-off
22 Diminutive endings
23 Restaurateur Toots
25 Stewart and Lovitz
27 Florida theme park
29 X-rated stuff
30 Garment line
33 "__ Gold" (Fonda film)
34 Banned apple spray
35 Actress Rogers
36 What this puzzle's perimeter contains abbreviations for
39 "Must've been something __"
40 Visa alternative, for short
41 Early Mexican
42 Chemical in Drano
43 Make a snarling sound
44 In pursuit of
45 Hockey's Jaromir __
46 Eau, across the Pyrenees
47 Dealer's wear
50 Wile E. Coyote's supplier
52 It's measured in minutes
55 Class clown's doings
57 Winter warmer
60 Farsi speakers
61 Summer cooler
62 Drink of the gods
63 Retired Mach I breaker

DOWN

1 When repeated, a Billy Idol hit
2 Give __ to (approve)
3 Monocle part
4 Sounds from a hot tub
5 Hogwash
6 2004 Will Smith film
7 "__ your instructions . . ."
8 More, in a saying
9 1970s–'80s supermodel Carangi
10 Playing hooky
11 Colorful salamanders
12 "Curses!"
13 Bring on board
14 Pet food brand
21 Discount apparel chain
23 Part of a shoot
24 Parasite's home
26 Sharer's pronoun
27 Former QB John
28 Former QB Rodney
29 More artful
30 Blackjack player's request
31 Mideast bigwig: Var.
32 Like items in a junk drawer: Abbr.
33 Gas, e.g.: Abbr.
34 Eritrea's capital
35 Mediterranean land
37 Yin's counterpart
38 Vegan's protein source
43 Deadhead icon
44 What many fifth graders have reached
45 Like some tax returns
46 BP gas brand
47 Self-absorbed
48 Concerning
49 Opposite of legato, in mus.
51 In vogue
52 Big name in desktop computers
53 Map line
54 Showed up
56 Ukr., once, e.g.
58 New Deal inits.
59 Conquistador's prize

by Samuel A. Donaldson

ACROSS

1 See 1-Down
5 Manages
10 Indolent
14 Wheel turner
15 Cognizant
16 Suffix with buck
17 "Out, damned ___!"
18 Perry Mason's secretary ___ Street
19 "Thumbnail" writings
20 What a broken-down car may get
21 Thick growth of trees
23 Former Ford compacts
25 Simian
26 Burden
27 Bullfighter
32 W.W. II-ending weapon, for short
34 Diamond or sapphire
35 Work ___ sweat
36 Actor Gyllenhaal of "Brokeback Mountain"
37 Four-bagger
38 Despot Idi ___
39 Bauxite or galena
40 Much of afternoon TV
41 Subsided
42 Voice between tenor and bass
44 Dispatched, as a dragon
45 1980s TV's "Emerald Point ___"
46 Old indoor light source
49 It's more than 90 degrees
54 Three on a sundial
55 Actress Loughlin of "Full House"
56 Harsh light
57 Sicilian peak
58 Door to the outside
59 Like certain cereals
60 Explorer Ponce de ___
61 Gold's and others
62 Seize (from)
63 Words of approximation

DOWN

1 With 1-Across, Coke vs. Pepsi competition, e.g.
2 Montreal baseballers, 1969–2004
3 Crockpot
4 Asian holiday
5 West Point students
6 Country singer Buck
7 Buddies
8 Writer ___ Stanley Gardner
9 Mariner
10 ___ tar pits
11 1997 Indy 500 winner ___ Luyendyk
12 Menageries
13 Dennis ___ and the Classics IV (1960s–'70s group)
21 Beat badly
22 German-made car since 1899
24 "This round's ___"
27 Home of Arizona State University
28 Has debts
29 Tray transporter
30 "The Andy Griffith Show" boy
31 Author Ayn
32 Do ___ on (work over)
33 Theda of early films
34 ___ of Arc
37 Lockup
38 Cain's victim
40 Depots: Abbr.
41 Women's magazine founded in France
43 Eskimos
44 Like 33-Down's films
46 Really mean people
47 Mythical king of Crete
48 Instrument for Rachmaninoff
49 Designer Cassini
50 Hardly streamlined, as a car
51 Fit
52 Banned orchard spray
53 ___ Dogg of R&B/hip-hop
57 "Do Ya" group, for short

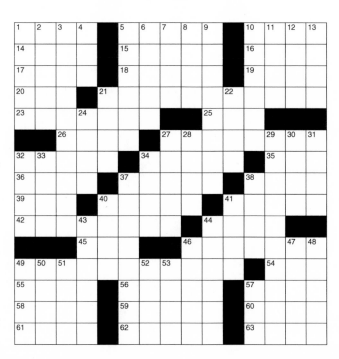

by Randy Sowell

ACROSS

1 Breezes through
5 Andrews and Edwards, for two: Abbr.
9 Wall supports
14 Blockhead
15 Zoo barrier
16 One getting one-on-one help
17 *Movie starring a cross-dressing John Travolta
19 Having a lot to lose?
20 In base 8
21 *Big writing assignment
23 Enjoyed Bazooka, e.g.
25 Carillon sounds
26 Lowly worker
28 ". . . ___ thousand times . . ."
29 Step up from dialup
32 Not at rest
36 Driver's license feature
38 Lab container
39 Word that can precede the starts of the answers to the eight starred clues
42 Lowell and Tan
43 The "A" in WASP
45 Is on deck
47 Most apts. have them
48 Strike caller
51 Wizard's stick
52 Places to serve slop
54 Flea market deal, perhaps
58 *Very easy tasks
62 Unable to retreat, as an animal
63 Fine fiddle
64 *Electric Slide, for one
66 Introductory TV episode
67 Author Bagnold
68 Not e'en once
69 Idyllic places
70 B'way booth in Times Square
71 Temperance supporters

DOWN

1 Like some committees
2 Alternative to first-class
3 Cream of the crop
4 *Nonbinding vote
5 Sound booster at a concert
6 Siege site
7 Called to a lamb, say
8 "Sophie's Choice" author
9 *Like a band-aid solution
10 Instruments in military bands
11 Lone Star State sch.
12 Dis and dis
13 Palm reader, e.g.
18 Winter driving hazard
22 6 on a telephone
24 The Everly Brothers' "All I Have to ___ Dream"
27 Japanese drama
29 Capitol feature
30 River of Hades
31 Not grasping the material, say
32 Lendl of tennis
33 Padre's boy
34 Rack purchases, briefly
35 Yuletide quaff
37 *Heels-over-head feat
40 Column crosser
41 Sign of sorrow
44 *Defeats mentally
46 Golf's Slammin' Sammy
49 Actress Farrow
50 Bit of shotgun shot
52 Determined to achieve
53 Long-bodied lizard
55 One of the Yokums
56 Cagney's TV partner
57 Close watchers
58 New Jersey's ___ May
59 In the thick of
60 Curly cabbage
61 Fit of pique
65 Publishers' hirees: Abbr.

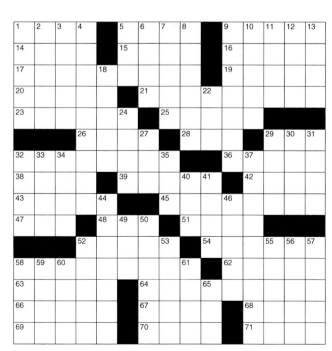

by Steve Dobis

ACROSS

1 This and that
6 Locale of famous playing fields
10 Start of the 13th century
14 Top of some forms
15 Whole lot
16 Obsessed mariner
17 Encyclopedia volume
18 Element number 55-Across
20 Bygone compact
21 Go carefully (over)
22 Dryer remains
23 Atlanta Brave who wore the number 55-Across
26 Done in
28 Halloween candy
29 Justification
30 Promising
34 Chemical suffix
35 President number 55-Across
38 It's a wrap
40 Cousin of a camel
41 Turn "this" into "_ . . . . ," e.g.
44 Earl Grey holder
48 Prefix with -hedron
49 Feb. 7, 2010, the date of this event's number 55-Across
52 Group of courses
53 Times in want ads
54 Cell material
55 See 18-, 23-, 35- and 49-Across
57 Steamy
59 Lake ___, discovery of Louis Jolliet
60 Lord over
61 Senseless
62 Absolutely
63 Melodramatic cry
64 Fireplace tool

DOWN

1 Snub
2 Musical liability
3 Brought to ruin
4 Charge
5 Transmit electronically
6 Calculator message
7 Bullish beginning?
8 A lot
9 Nonacademic degree
10 Capital founded by Spanish invaders, 1571
11 Sight from Taiwan
12 Admonishment
13 ThinkPad developer
19 If not
21 Music section
24 "American Idol" judge DioGuardi
25 Suffix with liquid
27 Santa Fe-to-Colo. Spr. direction
29 Sale sweeteners
31 Euro predecessor
32 Abbr. on a blotter
33 Truck scale unit
35 Study of Louis Pasteur
36 Stellar server
37 Old Dead Sea kingdom
38 Red or black, at a gaming table
39 Bar request
42 Held the floor
43 Tony winner Tyne
45 Apollo astronaut Frank
46 Deck cover
47 Forest clearings
49 1988 Olympics host
50 Palate part
51 Shimon of Israel
55 Ness, for one
56 Term of address in a monastery
57 Any of the Billboard Top 40
58 Game with Skip cards

by Richard Silvestri

ACROSS

1 Trap
6 Actress Stapleton of "All in the Family"
10 Way off
14 "The Goose That Laid the Golden Eggs" writer
15 The Bruins of the N.C.A.A.
16 ___ Valley, Calif.
17 "Portnoy's Complaint" author
19 Quick cut
20 Word after Web or camp
21 Geological stretch
22 Hosiery hue
23 Founder of the Christian Broadcasting Network
27 What oil cleanups clean up
30 Make ashamed
31 Silver or platinum
32 Italian and French bread?
34 Escape
37 "Duck soup!"
38 Promoters . . . or a description of 17-, 23-, 46- and 57-Across?
39 It may hold back the sea
40 Flight info
41 Twists out of shape
42 Russian revolutionary with a goatee
43 Old office note taker
45 Bank (on)
46 "Le Déjeuner des Canotiers" painter
50 Billy Crystal or Whoopi Goldberg for the Oscars, often
51 Perjure oneself
52 Currier's partner in lithography

56 "Phooey!"
57 He didn't really cry "The British are coming!"
60 Matured
61 Ferris wheel or bumper cars
62 Three wishes granter
63 Tennis do-overs
64 Poetical tributes
65 Willow for wicker

DOWN

1 Drains
2 Classic soft drink
3 With 41-Down, seemingly
4 Be a wizard or an elf, say, in Dungeons & Dragons
5 Prefix with center
6 One of 12 at a trial
7 Commercial prefix with Lodge
8 Computer key abbr.
9 "I'll pass"
10 Stock, bank deposits, real estate, etc.
11 Where winners are often photographed
12 Friend in a sombrero
13 Mature
18 No ___ Allowed (motel sign)
22 They're worn under blouses
24 The works
25 Reveals
26 Deep black
27 "Peter Pan" pirate
28 Mulching matter
29 "Mum's the word!"
32 Misplay, e.g.
33 Official behind a catcher
35 Related (to)
36 Repair
38 Window section
39 Takes away from, with "of"
41 See 3-Down
42 Luau gift
44 Stock analysts study them
45 Activist
46 Piano part
47 Concern of 38-Across
48 Escape from
49 "Frasier" character
53 Start of Caesar's boast
54 Buffalo's county
55 Clairvoyant
57 Golf lesson provider
58 Relief
59 Kind of trip for the conceited

by John Dunn

72

ACROSS

1 Leave in a hurry
7 Toothed tools
11 Where a truck driver sits
14 Swingline item
15 Field yield
16 Corrida cheer
17 *Impervious to picking, as a lock
19 Telecom giant acquired by Verizon
20 Legal ending
21 Leisure
22 Air apparent?
23 "Liquid diet" devotee
25 *Engraver's surface
28 Piled carelessly
30 Superlative suffix
31 Seized vehicle
32 High-rise apartment garden site
36 *Motto of the U.S. Coast Guard
40 Playful kissing
41 Middle-earth creatures
43 Catherine, the last wife of Henry VIII
45 Nestles
47 *Routine-bound bureaucrat
51 Online communications, for short
52 Notable times
53 Start the kitty
54 Tibetan beast
56 Rocker Ocasek
57 *Countries with big militaries
61 Part of a tuba's sound
62 Vietnam's continent
63 Naturally illuminated
64 Petal plucker's pronoun
65 Remain undecided
66 Compliment heard in the dress department

DOWN

1 Q-U connection
2 Hagen of Broadway
3 Camp clothing identifier
4 Antonyms: Abbr.
5 Lamb's coat
6 Not agin
7 Bit of fabric
8 Got out of bed
9 Affection seeker
10 Tanning lotion letters
11 '''''
12 "Little Women" author
13 It's darker than cream
18 Jalapeños and chilies
22 Rained pellets
23 Knight's title
24 Bills in tills
26 Hall's singing partner
27 Type size
29 Men of La Mancha
33 Sch. in Troy, N.Y.
34 Owner of a brand?
35 Debate the pros and cons
37 Sign of a contented cat
38 Improbable
39 Flower holder
42 Deflation sound
43 Persona non grata
44 Geronimo's tribe
46 Recover from a soaking
47 Those "walking" through the answers to the starred clues
48 YouTube button
49 Remove, as a corsage
50 Lieu
55 Barley beards
57 Knucklehead
58 Letter before omega
59 ___ Grande
60 "The ___ Erwin Show" of 1950s TV

by Paula Gamache

ACROSS

1 Sub for
6 Jungfrau or Eiger
9 Campaign against Troy, e.g.
14 Word after "thou"
15 Lighter maker
16 Bow, the "It Girl"
17 "Rikki-___-Tavi"
18 Mid 10th-century year
19 Tiny bits
20 Feature of a Las Vegas "bandit"
22 April 1 cigar sound
24 George Harrison's "___ It a Pity"
25 Do a Sherpa's work
27 24-line verse form
29 Toy on a layout
32 Water cannon target
33 Patch up
34 Nutrition label units
36 Branded beast
38 Lard holder
39 Kiltie's instrument
44 Huskies' sch.
46 Thing depicted by this puzzle's circled letters
47 "Night" novelist
51 Jet fuel component
54 Software buyer, usually
56 Kidney-related
57 "That was ___ . . ."
58 Tool at Henley
60 It beats the alternative, in a saying
63 Radio letter after sierra
65 Here-there link
67 Like porridge
68 Like SEALs
69 "That's not fair!"
70 Blast from the past
71 Architectural Digest topic
72 Pay stub abbr.
73 Items in a 46-Across, often

DOWN

1 Concerning
2 Place for a Vandyke
3 "Bye, now"
4 High-pH
5 Add while cooking
6 Multiple-choice choices
7 Life's partner
8 Place for a programming class, perhaps
9 Poli ___
10 Philippine seaport
11 Bothers no end
12 Starbucks size
13 Egg roll time
21 Ruler divs.
23 Old-time schoolteacher
26 "I ___ differ"
28 Daffy Duck trademark
29 One might pass for these, briefly
30 One down in the dumps?
31 Magician's prop
35 Daisy Mae's guy
37 Wishes undone
40 "Meet you then!"
41 Church dignitaries
42 Dark time, to a bard
43 Drop in on
45 '63 Liz Taylor role
47 Licked, e.g.
48 Yoga instructor's direction
49 Like paradise
50 Serenaded
52 Flying Cloud automaker
53 Like the art in some exhibits
55 Told in order to get a quick opinion
59 Cheer (for)
61 Heroic deed
62 Docs who might treat sinusitis
64 Key contraction
66 Axle, e.g.

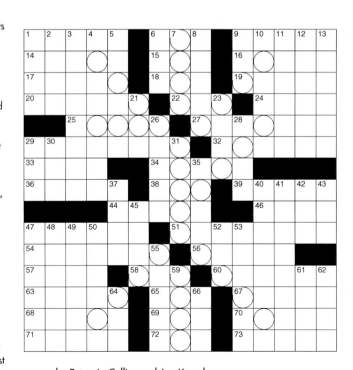

by Peter A. Collins and Joe Krozel

ACROSS

1 King Kong, e.g.
4 Trailer's connection to a car
9 Highly skilled
14 Where IVs may be administered
15 Japanese automaker
16 Theatrical medley
17 Emphatic south-of-the-border assent
19 Lessen
20 Comet, say, to the impressionable
21 Mocking remark
22 After-dinner candies
23 Central American canal locale
25 In great shape
26 Beginning piano student's exercise
33 Feeds, as pigs
37 Thing to hum or whistle
38 Neural transmitter
39 Vagrant
40 Test answer you have a 50/50 chance of guessing right
41 Nevada gambling mecca
42 Demon's doing
43 Nobelist Wiesel
44 Just sits around
45 Parting words
48 Finish
49 Prickly plant
54 No longer fashionable
57 Killer whale
60 United ___ Emirates
61 A-list
62 Wind that cools a beach
64 Aviator ___ Post
65 Word said upon answering a phone
66 Suffix with rocket or racket
67 Shop
68 Woody or Gracie
69 Banned bug spray

DOWN

1 See 8-Down
2 ___ donna (vain sort)
3 Ruhr Valley city
4 Contains
5 Winter river obstruction
6 Bluefin, for one
7 Wheat or soybeans
8 Loser to a tortoise, in a fable by 1-Down
9 Fragrance named for a Musketeer
10 Quick, cashless way to pay for things
11 "___ Almighty" (2007 movie)
12 Miniature golf shot
13 Gadgets not needed in miniature golf
18 "___ pig's eye!"
24 Roast hosts, for short
25 Costing nothing
27 The Beatles' "Any Time ___"
28 Roberts of "Erin Brockovich"
29 Beginning
30 Rink leap
31 The ___ Ranger
32 Outfielder Slaughter in the Baseball Hall of Fame
33 Kenny Rogers's "___ a Mystery"
34 Zero, in tennis
35 Village Voice award
36 Leisure suit fabric
40 Hatfield/McCoy affair
44 Ill temper
46 Cyclops feature
47 Give power to
50 ___ kwon do
51 Cornered
52 Vegged out
53 Roger with a thumbs-up or thumbs-down
54 Sunday seats
55 Touched down
56 Storage for forage
57 Workplace watchdog org.
58 Irish dance
59 Do some telemarketing
63 "Apollo 13" director Howard

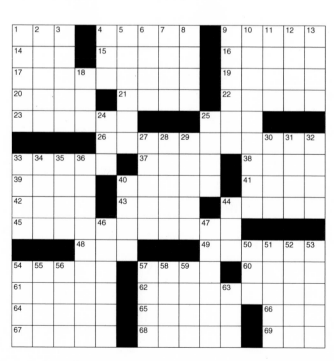

by Fred Piscop

ACROSS

1 Place for an oath
6 It's bugled on a base
10 Elevs.
14 Electron tube with two elements
15 Loads
16 Asia's shrunken ___ Sea
17 "Sharp Dressed Man" band
18 1970 Kinks song
19 TV explorer of note
20 Slapstick puppet show
23 Didn't bother
26 Guthrie at Woodstock
27 Baseball's Young and others
28 The Monkees' "___ Believer"
29 Kind of tide
31 Impress permanently
33 "I'm ready for anything!"
37 Centers of circles
40 Room at the top of stairs
41 Mideast fed.
42 Tacitus or Tiberius
43 Not a mainstream religion
44 Go get some shuteye
46 Prefix with pad
48 Mermaid's realm
49 Mail carrier's assignment: Abbr.
50 State of shock
52 Custard ingredients
55 Drink said to prolong life
57 Yuletide tune
60 Mercury or Saturn
61 Wise to
62 da-DUM, da-DUM, da-DUM
66 Tied
67 Je ne sais ___
68 Like redheads' tempers, supposedly
69 Villain in 2009's "Star Trek"
70 Bygone barrier breakers
71 Mystery writer's award

DOWN

1 Carpenter's tool with a curved blade
2 Eight-times-married Taylor
3 Tyke
4 Take on
5 Form of government Plato wrote about
6 Baby powder ingredient
7 Lei giver's greeting
8 ___ opposites
9 Co-creator of the Fantastic Four
10 Journey to Mecca
11 He said "Here's to our wives and girlfriends . . . may they never meet!"
12 Arriving after the bell, say
13 Wows at a comedy club
21 Classic brand of hair remover
22 E, in Morse code
23 Simpson and Kudrow
24 Ham it up
25 Magazine staffer
30 It has many needles
32 Bus. honchos
34 Toy you might enjoy while running
35 Basis for a Quaker cereal
36 Citi Field team
38 They have many needles
39 Worker on a comic book
42 Actuality
44 140 and up, say
45 Cad
47 Tennis umpire's cry
50 Some Madison Ave. workers
51 Drive drunkenly, perhaps
53 The "Homo" in "Homo sapiens"
54 "Tell me"
56 "In case you didn't hear me the first time . . ."
58 Casino game with Ping-Pong-like balls
59 Spanish liqueur
63 Computer unit, informally
64 Cup holder?
65 Leb. neighbor

by Caleb Madison

Celebrate the 100th Anniversary
of the Crossword Puzzle!

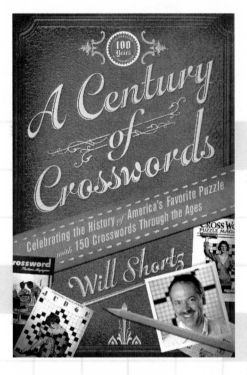

Available Summer 2013

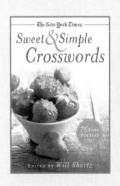

1

A	T	L	A	S		W	O	M	B		S	A	S	H
P	I	A	N	O		A	P	I	A		T	R	I	O
P	E	N	N	Y		D	U	N	G	A	R	E	E	S
	S	E	A	B	E	D	S		L	E	A	V	E	
		R	E	E	L		A	L	I	A	S	E	S	
G	A	R	B	A	G	E	T	R	U	C	K			
O	N	I	O	N		H	I	K	E		J	A	M	
B	O	O	R		C	R	U	D	E		H	I	D	E
I	D	S		L	O	O	M		A	I	M	A	T	
	B	A	S	E	B	A	L	L	G	A	M	E		
A	C	C	E	P	T	S		P	O	O	H			
T	R	A	C	E		M	E	G	A	T	O	N		
T	A	C	K	L	E	B	O	X		D	A	M	U	P
I	S	T	O		W	O	V	E		O	I	N	K	S
C	H	I	N		E	Y	E	S		F	L	I	E	S

2

R	A	F	T		C	C	C	P		S	L	O	B
I	N	L	A	W		A	L	O	E		H	A	R	E
M	A	O	R	I		D	E	N	T		A	S	I	A
	A	N	D	R	E	W	J	A	C	K	S	O	N	
S	O	T		T	O	N			R	E	I	N	S	
T	H	E	W	H	I	T	E	H	O	U	S	E		
A	I	R	E	S			M	O	R	E				
R	O	S	E		H	Y	P	E	R		A	S	A	P
			M	E	E	T			S	I	N	U	S	
	T	W	E	N	T	Y	D	O	L	L	A	R	S	
A	R	R	O	W			E	R	E		C	A	T	
D	O	U	B	L	E	S	A	W	B	U	C	K		
D	U	M	B		M	O	L	L		T	U	B	E	S
E	T	A	L		I	D	E	A		H	E	A	R	T
D	E	N	Y		R	A	S	P		D	R	A	Y	

3

A	B	C		O	T	H	E	R		A	S	B	A	D
G	R	O		D	R	A	M	A		T	H	A	N	E
H	I	P	J	O	I	N	T	S		H	O	D	G	E
A	B	S	O	R	B		P	R	O	P	J	E	T	
S	E	E	N		E	S	P		E	L	S	O	L	
T	D	S		I	C	E	A	G	E		K	I	A	
		S	N	A	P	J	U	D	G	M	E	N	T	
U	S	E	A	S		T	A	N		A	S	S	A	M
	S	T	U	M	P	J	U	M	P	E	R	S		
H	E	R		E	M	A	I	L	S		S	T	S	
	P	O	D	G	E		S	T	L		C	H	I	A
T	I	P	J	A	R	S		I	D	I	O	C	Y	
O	N	E	I	S		F	L	A	P	J	A	C	K	S
S	T	A	N	S		P	E	R	S	E		K	E	N
S	O	N	N	Y		D	O	M	E	D		S	R	O

4

A	L	T	O		W	R	O	T	E		V	E	S	T
J	O	H	N		H	A	G	A	R		E	C	H	O
A	G	E	R		A	N	D	R	E		G	O	A	D
R	O	Y	A	L	T	I	E	S		J	E	L	L	O
		M	O	S		N	I	N	E	T	I	E	S	
S	H	I	P	O	U	T		Y	E	A				
P	E	R		P	R	O	P	E	R	T	I	E	S	
E	X	I	S	T		O	B	E		S	E	A	L	Y
C	A	S	U	A	L	T	I	E	S		G	I	N	
		B	R	A		S	A	N	J	O	S	E		
B	E	A	U	T	I	E	S		M	I	O			
A	V	E	R	S		N	O	V	E	L	T	I	E	S
H	E	R	B		E	R	R	E	D		T	O	R	I
A	R	I	A		D	O	R	I	A		E	W	O	K
I	T	E	N		S	L	Y	L	Y		D	A	S	H

5

D	O	R	M	I		F	E	N	D	I		A	D	Z
E	P	E	E	S		A	L	I	E	N		R	I	A
F	A	R	M	A	N	I	M	A	L	S		K	E	G
A	Q	U	E	O	U	S		T	U	B	A			
N	U	N		A	L	A	S	K	A	R	A	N	G	E
G	E	S	S	O		L	E	O		E	B	S	E	N
		P	K	G		N	B	A		Y	A	N	G	
F	A	S	H	I	O	N	D	E	S	I	G	N	E	R
E	L	E	E		B	U	S		U	N	A			
A	L	A	R	M		D	U	B		S	P	A	C	Y
R	A	D	I	O	R	E	P	O	R	T		R	H	E
	E	C	R	U		O	P	I	A	T	E	S		
R	E	V		A	N	K	L	E	I	N	J	U	R	Y
A	L	I		S	T	E	E	R		C	A	R	R	E
Y	S	L		S	O	N	G	S		T	R	O	Y	S

6

```
S R T A S   E M U   D E F O G
Q U O T H   L A N   E L E C T
U N S H A C K L E   E L A T E
A L S   L O E W S   P A R
R E T O L D   A C T S   S A L
E T O N   G R O U P I N G S
      E P P I E   R A N O U T
A S P I R I N   I N C I T E S
S P E D U P   I N S E T
I R R A D I A T E   I S P S
S Y S   I T E S   S P O T O N
    E H S   R O O T S   A R A
I S I A H   A N D R E O T T I
M E D A L   T M I   U S U A L
S A S S Y   E E N   D U E L S
```

7

```
S C H   L E A D     J U S T I N
I R A   E P E E   S U P P O S E
T O S   V I S E   U N T I M E D
P U B L I C O P I N I O N
A C R O   P E T C O P A R K
T H O M A S   N A H   L E E S
    A C H E   L I K E   A R F
F R A N C I S C O P I Z A R R O
C O N   T A C O   S L R S
C A N T   A L A   N A P O L I
  M A R C O P O L O   E C O N
  U N D E R C O V E R C O P
O U T M O D E   O M E N   U M A
A V I A T E S   T P E D   R P I
T A N N E R   T A R S   S A N
```

8

```
A V E S   U S P S   F O C A L
B O R A   S O D A   A R U B A
F I R S T C L A S S C A B I N
A L O H A   S H O T   A D E
B A R I S T A   A L I G N E D
    M E A N T   I O N
R E G I S T E R E D N U R S E
A A A   N E A   B E G
P R I O R I T Y S E A T I N G
    W I S   S E T T E
S T E E P L E   L E T S S E E
H E S   P A P A   I T A L L
E X P R E S S C H E C K O U T
B A Y E R   O T O E   I N D O
A S S T S   M A I L   T E E N
```

9

```
S A B E R   T A D A   S P A R
T H R O E   E G O S   P A G E
R O U N D C H U C K   E Y R E
O R I   H A R E S   S E P A L
M A N D E L A   I T C H
    R A I N A L C O H O L
L U R I D   B E E P   N A B
A S A P   G L O S S   M E S A
W E D   Z O O M   F I S H Y
  R A V E R O B B E R S
    R I S E   I N A S T I R
A N G S T   B E G O T   O S E
X O U T   H O S T W R I T E R
E D N A   A L P O   O P E R A
L E S S   T O N E   W O M E N
```

10

```
H O P I   A D Z   R A D I A L
A M E N   D E A   O D E S S A
W O L F D O W N   P O P U P S
N O F A I R   I C E   Z E E
    M O N K E Y A R O U N D
C O D Y   G R A D E R
A B E   T A B   N O M I N E E
P O N Y U P   P I G O U T
P E T U N I A   R E X   N R A
    R E A G A N   S O O T
S Q U I R R E L A W A Y
H U T   I D I   H E R E T O
A R I S E S   B E A R U P O N
R A C I S T   I A M   P E R U
E N A C T S   S R O   Y E N S
```

11

```
R A W L S _ A M A T _ C A R R
A B O I L _ L O C H _ O G E E
D E R B Y _ A D U E _ N A L A
S T E R N U M S _ M A S T I C
_ _ A E R O _ B E S E E C H _
O D E S S A _ E A T E R _ _ _
B I V _ S N O R T _ A V A S T
I C E E _ O R I O N _ E L O I
S E N N A _ S T R E P _ E M O
_ _ A N J O U _ H O A X E S _
F A C T I O N _ C R O C _ _ _
O N R U S H _ F O U R T E E N
C Z A R _ A W A Y _ L I N D A
A I W A _ N O T E _ A V O I R
L O L L _ N E E R _ W E L T Y
```

12

```
E S P R I T _ Z A N E _ T A O
A T R I S K _ O D I N _ A D Z
T O O T H O F W O L F _ N R A
S A B U _ S L I P S O F Y E W
_ _ O A R _ Y E T _ L L A M A
E N S L E R _ _ _ A D O _ _ _
L U C _ E A S E U P _ A B O U
B L I N D W O R M S S T I N G
A L S O _ L O O S E N _ S E L
_ _ _ R D S _ _ _ S A S H A Y
O B A M A _ A A H _ G T O _ _
L I Z A R D S L E G _ A P B S
I T T _ W I T C H E S B R E W
V E E _ I D E O _ L O L I T A
E S C _ N O R A _ B R E C H T
```

13

```
P I T T _ A D V I L _ S O A R
A C H E _ M A I N E _ A H M E
R E E L _ A R S O N _ N E O N
_ _ B L Y N K E N A N D N O D
A M I _ O D E _ _ E A R N S _
L A R R Y A N D C U R L Y _ _
A U D I O _ _ R A N D _ _ _ _
W I S P _ A W A R E _ S S T S
_ _ _ E X A M _ C A C H E _ _
_ D E W E Y A N D L O U I E _
S T E N O _ _ O U I _ L S D _
C R A C K L E A N D P O P _ _
R E D O _ O C T A L _ U T A H
E V E R _ S H A M E _ S O H O
W I N E _ T O B E Y _ T R I O
```

14

```
S E C R E T _ M S P A C M A N
E L A I N E _ R H U B A R B S
G O D B L E S S A M E R I C A
A P E _ D E M _ A L S _ _ _ _
_ E T A L _ Z I T _ L A P I S
_ _ V I C _ T E A _ L I R A _
B E H I N D T H E S C E N E S
O R E _ D R E _ T H O _ O N S
R I G H T O N T H E M O N E Y
I C E E _ M E R _ S E X _ _ _
S A L A S _ T A J _ R O T C _
_ _ D A L _ G A G _ _ R O I _
P R E S B Y T E R I A N I S M
U N T U R N E D _ B A H A M A
B A D P E N N Y _ B A L L O T
```

15

```
S A A B _ T W O _ D A U N T S
A B B A E B A N _ A D R O I T
B A B Y T A L K _ B R I D E S
E C O L E _ D E B B I E _ _ _
R I T E _ R O Y A L F L U S H
_ _ _ A C E _ L E T _ P T A
_ N A V Y S E A L S _ S T U N
D O M E D _ S M A _ T H O N G
O N U S _ S K Y D I V I N G _
G E S _ G I E _ R A E _ _ _
S T E E L D R U M S _ L A N A
_ _ _ S I E S T A _ A D R E P
M T E T N A _ T H E B L U E S
R A T E D R _ E R A S A B L E
I N S E A M _ R E T _ W A Y S
```

16

```
PELE  EGAD  ACTOR
OXEN  SAGA  BLARE
SANTACRUZ   SALES
EMAIL PEZ   EPCOT
      RIM   LINT
 CHEVROLETCRUZE
DOO  ETNA  SEAMAN
IRMA  OPT   PAID
SEETHE ELEM  SRS
CARNIVALCRUISE
     ORAL   ASA
GESTE LAO  IGLOO
ELLIS WORKCREWS
ALAMO ENYA  EDNA
RAVEN TEXT  EASY
```

17

```
MELDS  JAYS   LAMP
UMIAK  ALEC   ERAS
SCARY  METAPHORS
KENNYG  IMEANIT
YEA  VACS  PERON
      MOLOKAI  FAD
IMBAD  SYR  RASTA
DRUNK  IFA  INKED
LOTSA  GAB  SAYSO
ECT   UNLINKS
 TILES LARY  YEP
HONORED  AMPERE
OBSESSION  OASIS
EEKS  UNDO  VNECK
DRYS  POET  ESSAY
```

18

```
AMPED  SAGAL  ETA
COREA  OLOGY  IOU
HOOKYLADDER  ERG
ESS  SOME  IWISH
DEY  POINTYSHOOT
  CLAM  TIETO
PIOUS  MENA  OHMY
MINTTEA  ARAPAHO
SISI  ARCS  PERON
    SERIA  SPED
PARTYPARCEL  YDS
ILOSE  TONI  FAN
ZIP  FAIRYSQUARE
ZEE  UNTIL  UNSER
AND  LOOPY  EATIT
```

19

```
AHORA  ROM   MASS
TENOR  INE  RESET
CHICKADEE  ONKEY
OHOH  CELTICS
SENECA  BUCKAROO
THY  ODS  PIA  APE
    SCION  BITER
 LACKADAISICAL
LUCIA  HOTLY
OLD  MOT  URL  APO
TUCKAHOE  EYELID
    AMMONIA  MLLE
PONZI  HUCKABEES
TAHOE  ORO  LEGOS
ARLO  TEN  ARENA
```

20

```
CAPRI  BLOC  BOWE
BRIAN  AERO  APEX
GELID  RAMP  KEPT
BALLOONPAYMENT
    AOL  NCOS
DISTRACT  ARARAT
OSU  FLOATPLANE
BANAL  ORB  HELIX
BANDOFGOLD  PST
SKIDOO  SEARCHES
   ERNS  WOO
 PARADEMAGAZINE
CURL  UNIX  DECAF
OPIE  ESME  INEPT
QUAY  SEED  ESTES
```

21

```
ODD   CRUMB   PLIES
NEE   HENIE   LATCH
ETA   ATRIA   AGILE
HEN   NIE  CSI  SAE
ENRAGES   HANDSIN
ATUB   TABU   RORY
RESETS   CUTEY
TSK   RESUMES   HAL
   HYATT   SEMITE
PEAS   NEED   ETTA
EXOTICA   OVERLAP
NPR  DEM  NOW  ICY
TOTAL   IRATE   SHE
ASIDE   EATER   TEA
DECOR   REEDS   SSR
```

22

```
DRAB   IRAS   TRAPP
OONA   DOME   WAXER
FINS   LAIC   ONICE
FLATTENSOUT   SKY
   EAR   SNAIL
AMS   DIP   DEMEANS
TUMS   CHER   EERIE
BLOWSHOTANDCOLD
ATTIC   NATO   HOLE
TIEGAME   END   MAR
   SLABS   SAM
STS   AVOTRESANTE
PAPAW   ORAN   DEAL
ALOHA   KEYS   AMIS
RETAG   SWEE   MOLE
```

23

```
ARAL   FOXY   HAFT
BONE   ODIE   EERIE
FLOG   TINA   LYCRA
ALLALONGTHE   SEM
BEDLAM   SECT
   ATAT   ATRAIN
WATCHTOWER   USNA
IRATE   FAS   STEEP
LILI   PURPLEHAZE
TACOMA   NATO
   NAPS   TIRADE
EMI   JIMIHENDRIX
BANJO   ELAN   ASAP
ARDOR   LINC   ROLE
NYSE   LADY   ENOL
```

24

```
BAGEL   URSA   OTIS
IRAQI   NOEL   AHME
XPLUSYISSIXTEEN
   ALE   ATEE   GAS
TRITEST   ENDORSE
SOME   YEATS   NAYS
OUI   TOSS   ETD
   XMINUSYISFOUR
   POT   ETAT   AOL
DART   METAL   STDS
IDEAMEN   SAUTEED
OMS   RARE   RNA
XISTENANDYISSIX
IRED   EGOS   TIETO
NEDS   REST   ESSEX
```

25

```
ABODE   FLINT   FOX
RUBES   RADAR   ATE
EXAMS   ABOLITION
TOME   APR   DCAREA
EMANCIPATION
   TAKETO   TSARS
CUBISM   SIM   MOO
ABRAHAM   LINCOLN
SEA   NAS   NEARLY
ARTOO   ROBINS
   PROCLAMATION
CAMEBY   ANE   LOVE
OFSLAVERY   ZOWIE
BRR   CELIA   STAND
BOP   HYMAN   ASSES
```

26

```
EERIE  TRAMP  GPA
SPURS  EASYA  OED
PINKPANTHER  LPS
 TRINI  BREADS
COIN  REGIS  RBIS
SMOG  WARN  BRUCE
TET  SARI  LOGON
  PURPLECOW
ACRID  LILT  BOO
TREKS  NERO  SEXY
MODE  CASES  TAIL
 UPROOT  ELAND
ITO  WHITERABBIT
RON  NAVEL  PLAZA
ANY  SNEAK  SEGER
```

27

```
DISMAY  MASK  TRY
ELAINE  OMNI  HIE
FOUNTAINPEN  ASA
ONCUE  DELE  RTES
GAYE  MITERJOINT
  TRA  SODS
ASH  EMAIL  CEASE
CHAMPAGNECOOLER
HALAL  ENNIS  LEG
 FRAU  TEL
HOKEYPOKEY  IRAN
OWNS  TUNA  ANIME
LEO  WATERINGCAN
ENT  OKRA  TOUCHE
SSS  NEED  SNAILS
```

28

```
COME  LAW  ASK
LOPEZ  SARA  DAIS
ELENI  TWIG  ABLE
TALON  ENDOWMENT
  REAP  NRA
CLASS  BASINETS
LEAH  ABEL  STARE
ALB  INOROUT  TEN
SLAYS  STER  MEAT
TONELESS  STAND
  SEN  BAAL
SANDSTONE  SALSA
ISEE  AREA  TBILL
TORA  IMET  EASEL
FOR  LED  DRAW
```

29

```
SMELL  SCULL  HOG
IGLOO  HOSEA  ACE
TRYTRYAGAIN  NEE
  TEMPS  DEGAS
CADENCE  SALTINE
ONOR  ARMENIAN
VINYL  ELAN  TSP
EST  IMITATE  HOE
YES  GAVE  SPEWS
 TIAMARIA  OREO
BOOKMAN  NIPPERS
RUPEE  PUREE
INN  NEVERSAYDIE
ECO  TOILE  LEARN
FEW  SNITS  ESSES
```

30

```
AARP  GLIB  ARSON
RIAL  OONA  QUEUE
USDA  SCAN  USERS
BLACKHAWK  ASI
AERIE  LEAH  ONES
  DIGS  BAG  GLO
GIGOLO  ELIA  RIB
URL  LAWYERS  ETE
TOA  OTHE  DODDER
ENS  REI  JOVE
NYSE  EZRA  ELATE
  WSJ  BUCKNAKED
RIATA  ALOU  YIPE
ARLEN  NEBR  ERIN
FALSE  GRIT  DADS
```

31

X	E	N	I	A		M	O	R	K		B	Y	R	D
A	L	O	N	G		O	N	E	I		L	E	A	N
N	I	E	C	E		R	E	A	D		U	L	N	A
D	O	N	A	L	D	R	U	M	S	F	E	L	D	
Y	T	D		I	R	O	N		M	G	M			
			A	M	Y	W	I	N	E	H	O	U	S	E
A	L	I	B	I		T	E	A		N	I	T	A	
N	O	N	S	T	O	P		O	L	D	D	E	A	R
E	C	T	O		S	O	W		O	A	S	T	S	
W	A	L	L	A	C	E	B	E	E	R	Y			
	U	N	U		Y	L	E	M		I	Z	E		
N	A	T	A	L	I	E	P	O	R	T	M	A	N	
B	E	B	E		A	B	A	A		O	A	S	I	S
A	R	A	L		T	I	T	S		O	T	E	R	O
R	O	S	Y		E	S	S	O		M	A	T	E	R

32

M	A	O		A	R	T	S		J	O	I	N	T	S
A	R	R	I	V	E	A	T		A	G	R	E	E	D
S	I	G	M	A	C	H	I		M	A	I	T	A	I
T	E	A	S		O	O	P	S		U	S	S	R	
S	S	N		K	N	E	E	H	I	G	H			
	M	O	I			N	U	D	E		M	D	S	
A	L	U	M	N	A		D	S	T		C	O	A	T
W	I	S	E	G	U	Y		H	A	I	R	D	Y	E
E	R	I	N		R	A	W		G	L	U	E	O	N
S	A	C		P	A	P	A		L	D	L			
			C	L	E	A	R	S	K	Y		P	R	E
L	I	S	A		T	H	E	O		A	L	O	T	
M	U	D	P	I	E		E	V	A	N	B	A	Y	H
I	N	L	A	N	D		R	E	L	I	A	N	C	E
A	G	E	N	T	S		O	R	A	L		E	E	L

33

G	R	A	S	P		B	A	S	E		A	Q	U	A
L	A	S	E	R		U	R	L	S		C	U	P	S
A	G	I	L	E		S	E	A	T		T	O	S	S
D	U	F	F	Y	S	T	A	V	E	R	N			
			O	I	L			O	O	H	E	D		
	F	I	N	N	E	G	A	N	S	W	A	K	E	
D	E	L			O	B	O	E		Z	I	A		
G	I	L	L	I	G	A	N	S	I	S	L	A	N	D
U	S	O		A	S	I	N			E	R	G		
M	C	N	A	M	A	R	A	S	B	A	N	D		
P	O	S	T	S			O	A	R					
		H	O	G	A	N	S	H	E	R	O	E	S	
A	S	E	A		I	T	O	O		T	E	R	R	A
L	A	W	N		G	O	T	O		H	A	S	I	D
A	X	E	D		S	P	A	N		A	L	O	N	E

34

A	P	E	R	S			S	I	R	E		R	E	P
R	O	D	E	O		I	N	N	E	R		A	G	E
R	I	D	D	L	E	C	A	K	E	S		I	R	A
			T	I	M	O	R		K	E	R	N	E	L
M	I	R	A		I	N	L	A	W		C	A	T	S
O	N	A	P	A	R			L	E	G	A	L		
N	A	V	E	L		M	O	T	E	L		C	A	M
E	N	E		P	R	O	V	O	K	E		O	R	E
T	E	N		H	U	L	A	S		A	S	H	E	N
		I	P	A	N	A			S	N	O	O	T	S
A	L	M	A		T	R	A	L	A		P	L	E	A
M	E	A	D	O	W		L	I	N	E	R			
B	A	G		R	O	W	I	N	G	P	A	I	N	S
E	V	E		C	R	A	C	K		I	N	D	I	E
R	E	S		S	K	Y	E			C	O	O	P	T

35

B	L	A	M	E		P	E	R	T		C	E	L	L
R	O	L	E	S		I	C	E	R		A	Q	U	A
A	G	E	N	T		C	O	P	A		S	U	M	O
T	O	S	S	A	S	A	L	A	D		T	I	P	S
			A	T	T	Y		S	E	G	A			
A	C	T		E	R	U	P	T		A	V	A	S	T
B	R	E	T		I	N	A		L	O	O	K	M	A
B	A	T	H		P	E	T	C	O		T	I	E	S
A	Z	O	R	E	S		C	R	O		E	T	A	T
S	Y	N	O	D		C	H	E	F	S		A	R	E
			W	A	S	H		S	A	P	S			
B	A	J	A		P	I	T	C	H	A	T	E	N	T
O	L	A	F		I	S	E	E		C	A	M	E	O
R	A	V	I		T	O	R	N		E	V	I	A	N
G	N	A	T		E	X	I	T		K	E	R	R	Y

36

L	A	U	D	E	D	■	L	A	I	■	S	M	E	E
E	L	N	I	N	O	■	I	N	K	■	T	A	T	A
A	D	D	S	T	O	■	S	T	E	W	A	R	D	S
P	E	A	C	H	F	U	Z	Z	■	A	N	G	S	T
T	R	Y	■	R	U	S	T	■	M	R	T	■	■	■
■	■	H	O	S	S	■	D	A	S	H	I	N	G	■
A	L	I	E	N	■	T	O	U	R	■	E	S	A	U
P	U	P	A	E	■	E	T	S	■	K	M	A	R	T
S	L	O	T	■	J	E	T	T	■	A	A	N	D	E
O	L	D	S	O	U	L	■	M	A	N	N	■	■	■
■	■	T	N	T	■	R	O	E	G	■	A	D	S	■
C	A	I	R	O	■	C	O	P	S	A	P	L	E	A
A	L	S	O	R	A	N	S	■	O	R	I	G	I	N
P	E	A	K	■	A	B	E	■	P	O	L	I	C	E
P	E	K	E	■	A	C	S	■	S	O	L	D	E	R

37

B	O	L	E	■	R	C	A	S	■	J	E	S	S	E
O	P	E	N	W	E	A	V	E	■	E	T	A	T	S
C	A	T	C	H	E	S	G	L	I	T	C	H	E	S
A	L	S	■	A	L	B	■	A	N	S	E	L	M	O
■	■	B	R	E	A	■	S	U	E	T	■	■	■	■
S	C	R	A	T	C	H	E	S	I	T	C	H	E	S
T	O	O	H	O	T	■	S	I	T	■	A	L	A	■
U	C	O	N	N	■	I	T	E	■	A	D	R	A	G
M	O	S	■	R	N	A	■	A	R	I	S	T	A	■
P	A	T	C	H	E	S	B	R	I	T	C	H	E	S
■	■	H	I	V	E	■	O	M	I	T	■	■	■	■
A	N	T	I	G	U	A	■	U	H	S	■	S	R	A
M	A	T	C	H	E	S	S	T	I	T	C	H	E	S
A	T	O	L	L	■	O	N	E	G	A	T	I	V	E
D	O	P	E	Y	■	N	O	S	H	■	N	A	S	A

38

J	A	M	B	■	E	M	I	L	■	A	R	M	E	D
E	S	A	I	■	R	E	N	O	■	L	E	O	N	A
S	I	N	G	L	E	O	C	C	U	P	A	N	C	Y
T	A	E	B	O	■	W	H	I	R	■	S	O	S	■
■	■	A	L	S	■	G	O	O	■	■	■	■	■	■
D	O	U	B	L	E	I	N	D	E	M	N	I	T	Y
I	T	T	Y	■	E	D	I	E	■	A	S	T	R	A
G	T	E	■	S	P	E	N	C	E	R	■	I	A	L
A	E	R	I	E	■	A	J	A	X	■	A	N	N	I
T	R	I	P	L	E	L	A	Y	E	R	C	A	K	E
■	■	L	A	T	■	S	A	C	■	■	■	■	■	■
■	S	H	E	■	T	A	C	K	■	C	E	L	I	A
Q	U	A	D	R	U	P	L	E	B	Y	P	A	S	S
V	E	R	G	E	■	E	U	R	O	■	T	O	N	I
C	R	E	E	D	■	X	E	N	A	■	S	S	T	S

39

H	T	T	P	■	S	O	L	E	■	S	C	U	F	F
E	I	R	E	■	A	V	O	W	■	T	O	R	R	E
R	A	I	N	■	R	A	R	E	■	A	R	N	A	Z
B	R	O	C	C	O	L	I	R	A	B	E	■	■	■
S	A	S	H	A	Y	S	■	P	L	A	T	E	S	■
■	■	A	L	A	■	O	D	I	E	■	A	L	P	■
R	U	N	N	I	N	G	B	E	A	R	■	T	I	E
A	T	I	T	■	E	O	E	■	R	U	H	R	■	■
K	I	X	■	B	A	R	E	M	I	N	I	M	U	M
E	C	O	■	O	H	M	S	■	M	E	G	■	■	■
S	A	N	D	R	A	■	O	P	I	A	T	E	S	■
■	■	R	E	B	A	M	C	E	N	T	I	R	E	■
L	I	V	E	D	■	M	O	E	T	■	O	B	I	E
A	M	I	G	O	■	F	R	A	U	■	N	E	C	K
S	P	A	S	M	■	M	E	N	S	■	I	R	A	S

40

B	I	O	L	■	B	O	S	C	H	■	M	A	C	E
R	A	R	E	■	O	R	T	H	O	■	A	L	A	S
E	M	A	G	■	B	R	E	E	D	S	H	I	L	L
A	N	N	U	L	S	■	W	A	S	H	O	■	■	■
D	O	G	M	A	■	S	A	P	■	A	G	A	T	E
S	T	E	E	R	■	T	R	O	U	■	A	L	M	A
■	■	■	E	D	I	T	■	T	E	N	D	E	R	■
E	C	U	A	D	O	R	■	M	A	R	Y	A	N	N
G	A	S	L	O	G	■	A	S	H	E	■	■	■	■
A	R	I	L	■	S	E	V	E	■	S	H	E	E	P
L	E	A	S	T	■	M	O	C	■	T	I	L	D	E
■	■	I	O	N	I	C	■	R	U	D	E	S	T	■
N	E	W	Z	E	A	L	A	N	D	■	E	V	E	S
F	R	E	E	■	S	I	D	E	A	■	H	E	L	I
L	A	B	S	■	H	O	O	T	S	■	I	N	S	T

41

S	L	E	D		A	L	M	S			D	A	Z	E	D
P	E	P	E		L	E	A	H			O	B	A	M	A
E	G	O	S		I	A	G	O			M	A	G	U	S
W	A	X	I	N	G	P	O	E	T	I	C				
S	L	Y		U	N	T	O		E	N	I	G	M	A	
		A	L	E			S	A	G		L	E	X		
	F	U	L	L	D	I	S	C	L	O	S	U	R	E	
E	L	L	A			B	O	O			L	E	I	S	
W	A	N	I	N	G	I	N	T	E	R	E	S	T		
E	R	A		I	R	S			R	A	W				
S	E	R	E	N	E		S	O	U	P		M	A	R	
		N	E	W	H	A	M	P	S	H	I	R	E		
A	B	C	T	V		A	B	E	T		E	N	T	S	
T	U	T	E	E		U	R	G	E		L	E	O	I	
M	Y	R	R	H		L	E	A	D		M	O	O	N	

42

F	R	I	S	K		Z	A	C	K		A	S	E	A	
W	I	C	C	A		U	P	O	N		C	U	L	T	
D	O	E	R	R		L	E	V	I		C	A	V	E	
	T	R	E	A	S	U	R	E	T	R	O	V	E	S	
			W	O	N				W	I	S	E	S	T	
T	R	I	C	K	O	R	T	R	E	A	T				
N	O	V	A	E		H	A	H	A	S		M	M	E	
U	T	E	P		T	I	M	O	R		J	O	E	L	
T	O	S		W	A	N	E	D		A	E	O	N	S	
			T	R	I	E	D	A	N	D	T	R	U	E	
S	O	L	E	I	L				E	M	B				
T	R	A	C	T	O	R	T	R	A	I	L	E	R		
R	A	S	H		R	O	M	A		R	A	R	E	R	
A	T	T	N		E	W	A	N		E	C	L	A	T	
P	E	S	O		D	A	N	G		S	K	E	D	S	

43

C	A	B	O	T		D	A	B	S		C	A	S	H	
A	L	E	R	O		E	L	L	E		A	L	A	S	
L	O	R	I	S		E	D	O	M		N	E	X	T	
L	U	N	G	C	A	P	A	C	I	T	Y				
		A	A	R	P				H	O	U	S	E		
S	K	I	M		C	U	R	T	A	I	N	R	O	D	
M	A	G	I	C		R	A	R	E	R		A	L	I	
I	B	N		E	M	P	R	E	S	S		N	A	T	
T	O	O		T	A	L	I	A		T	R	U	C	E	
H	O	R	S	E	S	E	N	S	E		U	S	E	D	
S	M	E	A	R				O	N	C	D				
		M	A	I	D	E	N	V	O	Y	A	G	E		
U	M	P	S		T	O	R	O		N	A	S	A	L	
Z	E	R	O		E	S	A	U		G	R	I	N	S	
I	R	O	N		M	E	S	S		A	D	A	G	E	

44

M	Y	S	T		C	A	S	T		S	P	A	M	
R	O	T	O	R		O	B	E	Y		E	R	G	O
B	U	R	M	A		R	A	C	K	E	T	E	E	R
U	R	I		I	M	P			E	X	T	E	N	T
R	E	C	K	L	E	S	S			C	O	N	D	O
N	I	T	E		T	E	C	H	I	E		S	A	N
S	T	E	V	E			H	A	L	L	S			
		R	I	C	K	R	O	L	L	I	N	G		
			N	O	O	I	L			N	O	E	L	S
H	A	M		C	O	B	A	L	T		B	R	E	T
A	R	U	B	A			R	O	C	K	S	T	A	R
R	O	S	A	R	Y			O	U	I		R	K	O
R	U	C	K	S	A	C	K	S		S	Q	U	A	B
I	S	L	E		W	H	E	E		S	E	D	G	E
S	E	E	R		S	I	G	N			D	E	E	S

45

	S	P	E	E	D		L	I	L	T		Z	E	A	L
	A	L	I	K	E		I	N	O	R		A	L	T	A
	Ⓙ	A	G	G	E	Ⓓ	E	D	G	E		I	L	E	S
	A	C	H		P	Ⓞ	N	Y	E	Ⓧ	P	R	E	S	S
	K	E	T	T	L	E	S			L	E	N	T	O	
			B	O	Y	S		B	A	L	E				
	B	R	A	T			D	O	G	P	Ⓐ	D	D	L	E
	L	O	L	A		M	E	N	U	S		R	I	O	T
	Ⓣ	O	L	L	P	L	Ⓐ	Z	A			I	S	T	O
				E	B	R	O			I	K	E	S		
	A	S	T	A	R				A	T	E	D	I	R	T
	M	A	R	Ⓒ	U	S	W	E	L	Ⓑ	Y		D	E	O
	O	X	E	N		H	I	D	D	E	N	G	E	M	S
	R	O	V	E		A	N	N	E		E	R	N	I	E
	E	N	I	D		G	E	A	R		S	E	T	T	E

46

```
M G S   P A N D A S   P F F T
E L O   O B O I S T   E R I E
G O U N D E R T H E K N I F E
  B L A S T   T E R I   S T N
C A M P   B O R N W I T H A
B L U E I C E     A I R
S I S   N I E C E     A S S
  S I L V E R S P O O N I N
  M C I   S T O N E   D A S
    P A C   C O N C E P T
O N E S M O U T H   H O P E
F A N   B A B E   M O O R E
F O R K I T O V E R B U D D Y
A M O I   E L Y S E E   E T A
L I N T   S T E A D Y   R O Y
```

47

```
J O U S T   J O E Y   J O S H
O P R A H   E N N E   A R E A
J E S S E J A M E S   N E A T
O L A   M A N Y   I D I O T S
    J A Y S   T K O S
  A B A S E   H U N G J U R Y
S L A C K   M E N O   O N E A
E L M O   J C R E W   P I N K
R O B B   E G O S   P L O T S
F R I J O L E S   G A I N S
    A B L E   M A N N
H A R V E Y   F A L A   A L I
A L A I   J O E J A C K S O N
H U R T   A L T O   H I T O N
A M E S   R E A R   E X A M S
```

48

```
T A C O   S M A R T   A B R A
A L A N   P U S H Y   B E E P
T I N K E R S H O R T S T O P
A T A P R I C E   R O A S T
    A T L   L I A R
E V E R S S E C O N D B A S E
N E R V E   H O N E   S P A
I T I S   T R I M S   S P I T
A C C   O R E L   S I C E M
C H A N C E F I R S T B A S E
    U T E S   E T O
O B A M A   B R A I N I A C
D O U B L E P L A Y C O M B O
D A R E   G O T T I   M A L T
S T A R   O L S E N   E X E S
```

49

```
D I T S   E V E R   C O B R A
E V R Y   M A X I   A D O U T
M A I N   B L A C K P E A R L
O N A   D E S C E N T
T O G A E D   T R I   K E E L
E V E N T   M A S T   I M N O
    N A P A S   T A K I N G
A S T A I R E   R E W I R E S
D I A B L O   N O R A D
A T I E   B O O M   R E M I T
H U L L   L O S   I D E A T E
    P E L T E R S   S R S
S A N T A M A R I A   S A I L
O D E O N   L I N T   P L E A
Y E G G S   A L E E   F A D S
```

50

```
M A S K   H U M U S   E F O R
U N T O   U N A P T   T R I O
S C A R   S A Y N O   H E L D
T H R E S H   B E M I N E
D O R A T H E E X P L O R E R
O R Y   P U P   T S E   I W O
    K A S E M     A D E N
  J O E T H E P L U M B E R
H U N G     H E N C E
A D E   S A C   E T D   A L A
R O S I E T H E R I V E T E R
  L O C K I N   T I N H A T
I S I N   I N T E L   D O P E
D E C I   N U R S E   E M I R
E X E C   S P E E D   D E N Y
```

51

```
I C E R S   T O M B   D E A F
S A M O A   I N G A   U C A L
P R I M P   G I R D   L O R I
S T R A I G H T   G A L L O N
      N E A T   C U N N I N G
S T R O N G   C L Y D E
A H A   S E A L E   A S H E S
W I S E   S P E A K   S I C K
S N A C K   S A N E R   G H I
      L O S E R   N A C H O S
S I M I L E S   B A N A
O N A P A R   S L I P P E R Y
L U G S   A S T I   A T R I A
I S M E   P E E N   S O B E R
D E A D   H A R D   T R E N D
```

52

```
N I N E   O L A N   P A S S E
O N O R   T I N E   E M P T Y
L A M A   T O N E   S M I T E
E T A S   O N U S   T O R E
S I N E W   L O G   I R A
S E S S I L E   N A P S T E R
      S O R E   L A T E S T
S T A N D A R D W O R K D A Y
P E R I O D   S O R T
I S T H M U S   P E E V I S H
N T H   P C B   D O L C E
  F O R T   O R B S   I L E X
C L U E R   F O R E   D I N O
O E S T E   F I R E   O N E S
S W E D E   S L R S   F I V E
```

53

```
L A L A   J E T S   O R B I T
E T A S   A R O N   D E L C O
G E T T I N G C O L D F E E T
I M H I P   S K O A L   S S T
O P E N E D   T W O   S H E
N O R   C U E S   S T A Y E R
    H A N D I N   T O E S
  C H I C K E N I N G O U T
F O A L   N A T I O N
E R R O R S   I S B N   E M I
R N A   A O K   S E A M A N
U P S   I N R E D   I T E R S
L O S I N G O N E S N E R V E
E N E R O   N O A H   A G E R
S E D A N   A L L Y   M E L T
```

54

```
B I D E N   C L I O   O N A N
A D A N O   A E R O   R E L Y
D O N T M O V E A M U Z Z L E
F I G   S C I   P R O P S
I D E D   T A R S A L   E T A
T O R I C   R I C H   W R A P
    T U B   N A P   E C R U
  B U Z Z I N G T A B L E S
K A T E   T E L   H A L
I S I S   O M E N   R E C U R
D S L   P H O T O N   S A S E
  T I E T O   L E S   M E D
F U Z Z A N D F E A T H E R S
U B E R   E Y E S   E E R I E
N A D A   Y E W S   P R A D A
```

55

```
C P A S   S L O P   C U F F S
H E M P   T O N E   U T I L E
A R E A C O D E S   P E R O N
R U N N I N G A T A B   E S T
    K N E E L   M O S E S
M R D E E D S   I B A R S
G O O D   O V E R A C T S
M A N   K E Y W O R D   A H H
T R O P I C A L   B P O E
  T E N O R   D E B E E R S
  D E I G N   D O P E S
T I N   L O S E C O N T R O L
S A T I E   U P I N S M O K E
A N E R A   M O L Y   A X I S
R A R E R   S T E M   N Y E T
```

56

```
L A K E   H E M P   G A M M A
I D E S   O B I E   A V I A N
S H E S A L A D Y   Z E S T Y
T O N E R   N I O B E
S C E N T S     T A B A S C O
    Y O U R E S O V A I N
C A P S   P R E   S A L T S
A N I N   S N E R D   I S E E
V I S O R   V E E   L A S T
I M A B E L I E V E R
L E N S M E N   R E C T O R
    N A C H O   A L I V E
J A B B A   H E S A R E B E L
A L I E N   E L L Y   A I R E
B E N E T   S L O E   T A T E
```

57

```
T A N   E R U P T   B A B A R
A S A   R A T I O   A R U B A
D I S A R M A N D H A M M E R
A F A R   S H A D E   A P S E
      A T E     R O N
D I S M I S S A M E R I C A
A N T I C   M O O S E   A V E
T K O S   B E R R Y   S P A T
E E L   N E A T O   M A R I A
  D I S B A R A N D G R I L L
      A C T     A R T
I M A M   O A T E R   R I L E
D I S B A N D O N T H E R U N
O C E A N   I N N E R   A M Y
L E A S T   N E E D S   S P A
```

58

```
C U B S   D I V A   F U Z Z Y
U S O C   E M I T   O K I E S
R E F I   A N E W   R E P E L
B U F F A L O W I N G S
S P O I L S   L E I   I D O
    L I L Y L I V E R E D
E D N A   N A E   N E G A T E
T R U R O   G M S   N O N E T
A L B I N O   E U R   S I R S
T A B L E T E N N I S
S O Y   C O X   D A Y S P A
    J U S T A D D W A T E R
N A B O B   O P A L   C A S T
O M A N I   L O D E   H I T S
D I G I T   S P A R   T R O Y
```

59

```
C A S H   D E B R A   F E S T
A C L U   E N T E R   A M I E
C R U M B C R U S T   J A G S
T E M P E R A S   D W I G H T
I S P   R I G   B E A T
    C R E E P Y C R A W L Y
E N J O Y S   A T O M   H U E
P E A T   I C E   D A T A
I A N   L A N E   S A U T E S
C R E D I T C R U N C H
    R O T H   S O T   R P I
B A N A N A   R A W O N I O N
A G O G   C R A B C R E O L E
R E D O   K U K L A   A T O P
E D E N   S T E E P   P S S T
```

60

```
C Z A R   M A T H   F E S T
R E L O   R A D I O   O N C E
O R E O   E X U L T   O L A N
C O C K T A I L   T A T A R S
      S O D   T A I L P I P E
U T E   L E S   R E A R
P I P E D R E A M   S I T O N
S N I P   S L Y L Y   N O P E
Y A C H T   D R E A M T E A M
    E U R O   T R A   S L O
T E A M G A M E   D D E
I M M E S H   G A M E C O C K
N A I R   R E A V E   A M A N
G I G A   A R D E N   R O B E
E L A L   H E S S   D O S E
```

61

A	R	M	A	N	D	■	E	M	B	A	R	■	P	F	C
B	E	A	V	E	R	■	V	E	R	S	E	■	A	O	L
A	P	T	I	T	U	D	E	T	E	S	T	■	L	U	X
F	R	E	S	H	M	A	N	S	E	N	A	T	O	R	■
T	O	Y	■	U	S	S	■	■	M	A	M	I	E		
■	S	O	P	H	O	M	O	R	E	J	I	N	X		
S	N	O	W	■	U	R	N	■	N	O	T				
■	C	O	L	L	E	G	E	S	T	A	T	I	O	N	■
D	O	O	■	R	A	P	■	E	S	S	E				
J	U	N	I	O	R	P	A	R	T	N	E	R	■		
S	T	E	N	T	■	B	A	I	■	S	A	P			
■	S	E	N	I	O	R	D	I	S	C	O	U	N	T	S
A	I	L	■	T	H	E	I	M	M	O	R	T	A	L	S
M	G	S	■	I	N	A	N	E	■	L	E	E	R	A	T
I	N	E	■	S	O	R	E	N	■	A	S	S	E	S	S

62

Z	E	R	O	■	B	O	W	S	■	S	L	A	B
A	X	E	S	■	O	L	E	O	■	C	O	R	E
P	I	N	T	■	O	L	I	N	■	A	V	I	D
S	T	E	E	L	M	A	G	N	O	L	I	A	S
■	■	R	O	B	■	H	E	M	A	N	■		
J	I	B	■	T	O	A	S	T	S	■	G	T	O
A	D	A	P	T	O	R	■	S	C	A	T		
B	I	G	M	O	M	M	A	S	H	O	U	S	E
B	O	G	S	■	S	T	O	P	P	E	R		
A	M	Y	■	G	R	O	P	E	S	■	S	R	I
■	J	A	N	E	T	■	R	E	S	■	■		
P	R	E	L	U	D	E	T	O	A	K	I	S	S
R	E	A	L	■	A	L	A	I	■	I	N	L	A
A	N	N	O	■	C	L	O	D	■	R	O	O	F
M	O	S	T	■	T	O	S	S	■	T	R	E	E

63

S	W	A	P	■	P	A	R	T	B	■	D	A	M
R	O	W	E	D	■	I	T	I	S	I	■	O	R	E
T	R	A	D	E	S	C	H	O	O	L	■	T	E	A
A	S	K	■	C	U	S	S	■	L	O	M	A	N
S	T	E	E	L	E	■	D	A	N	Z	A	■		
■	B	A	R	T	E	R	S	Y	S	T	E	M		
I	K	N	O	W	■	W	R	O	T	E	■	R	D	A
S	P	A	N	■	D	I	A	N	A	■	V	I	D	I
L	A	N	■	M	A	N	S	E	■	S	I	X	A	M
E	X	C	H	A	N	G	E	R	A	T	E	■		
■	Y	O	R	K	E	■	N	E	W	A	G	E		
D	I	D	O	K	■	S	A	K	E	■	N	O	G
D	O	R	■	S	W	I	T	C	H	P	L	A	T	E
A	W	E	■	U	B	O	A	T	■	S	A	M	M	S
Y	A	W	■	P	A	N	G	S	■	M	E	E	T

64

J	A	B	■	C	O	R	G	I	■	A	M	T	O	O
A	L	E	■	O	D	E	O	N	■	B	I	E	R	S
C	I	R	■	B	O	A	R	D	■	O	X	E	Y	E
K	E	E	P	O	N	L	O	R	R	Y	I	N	■	
U	N	T	I	L	■	U	A	E	■	T	I	C	S
P	S	S	T	■	C	O	N	G	A	Q	U	E	U	E
■	■	A	L	O	U	D	■	U	P	S	E	T		
H	A	M	■	O	P	T	■	A	M	I	■	T	D	S
E	L	U	T	E	■	E	X	U	D	E	■		
W	I	S	E	B	L	O	K	E	S	■	L	I	M	P
N	E	I	N	■	A	C	E	■	V	I	D	E	O
■	C	A	T	C	H	S	O	M	E	Z	E	D	S
H	U	B	B	A	■	R	O	T	O	R	■	A	L	I
A	R	O	L	L	■	E	U	R	O	S	■	L	E	T
P	I	X	E	L	■	S	T	O	N	E	■	S	Y	S

65

S	T	E	V	E	■	J	A	C	K	■	I	B	M
E	R	R	O	R	S	■	A	L	E	E	■	N	E	A
C	O	N	A	N	O	B	R	I	E	N	■	J	A	Y
T	D	S	■	I	N	A	G	E	S	■	L	E	N	O
■	■	L	E	S	S	O	N	■	A	E	S	I	R
M	I	M	I	■	I	N	T	I	M	A	T	E	S
A	T	P	E	A	C	E	■	O	N	E	■		
J	O	H	N	N	Y	■	■	C	A	R	S	O	N
■	■	T	A	M	■	D	E	N	E	U	V	E	
A	B	O	M	I	N	A	T	E	■	S	N	A	G
S	O	L	O	S	■	G	I	B	E	A	T	■	
H	O	S	T	■	R	E	D	U	C	E	■	P	R	O
T	H	E	■	T	O	N	I	G	H	T	S	H	O	W
O	O	N	■	A	N	T	E	■	O	N	T	I	M	E
N	O	S	■	P	A	A	R	■	A	L	L	E	N

66

```
M I C   T O N I   I M P A L E
I N A   I D I D   N A R N I A
S K I L O D G E   G L I D E S
S E R E   S H O R E L E A V E
M Y O P I A   O M A R
      E A R P   M A R   A R F
S N O W L E O P A R D   J O E
T A B   M A N     A P R
A T E   S O P H I A L O R E N
B O Y   H U E   A T O P
      Y E T I   A G E N T S
S P E E D L I M I T   R O A N
C A N A D A   S R I L A N K A
A N D R E W   G A L E   O E R
M E S S R S   S E T S   S N L
```

67

```
M A L A R I A L   G A N D H I
O N E H O R S E   I B E R I A
N O N S T O P S   A S W A R M
Y D S     B E S T   E T T E S
      S H O R   J O N S
   E P C O T   S M U T   H E M
U L E E S   A L A R   M I M I
T W E N T Y S I X S T A T E S
I A T E   A M E X   O L M E C
L Y E   G N A R   A F T E R
      J A G R   A G U A
V I S O R   A C M E     A R C
A N T I C S   H O T C O C O A
I R A N I S   I C E C R E A M
N E C T A R   C O N C O R D E
```

68

```
T E S T   C O P E S   L A Z Y
A X L E   A W A R E   A R O O
S P O T   D E L L A   B I O S
T O W   D E N S E F O R E S T
E S C O R T S     A P E
   O N U S   T O R E A D O R
A B O M B   J E W E L   U P A
J A K E   H O M E R   A M I N
O R E   S O A P S   E B B E D
B A R I T O N E   S L E W
   N A S     O I L L A M P
O B T U S E A N G L E   I I I
L O R I   G L A R E   E T N A
E X I T   O A T E N   L E O N
G Y M S   W R E S T   O R S O
```

69

```
A C E S   A F B S   S T U D S
D O L T   M O A T   T U T E E
H A I R S P R A Y   O B E S E
O C T A L   T E R M P A P E R
C H E W E D   D O N G S
   P E O N   N O A   D S L
I N M O T I O N   P H O T O
V I A L   S H O R T   A M Y S
A N G L O   G O E S N E X T
N O S   U M P   W A N D
   S T I E S   R E S A L E
C A K E W A L K S   A T B A Y
A M A T I   L I N E D A N C E
P I L O T   E N I D   N E E R
E D E N S   T K T S   D R Y S
```

70

```
S T U F F   E T O N   M C C I
L I N E A   R A F T   A H A B
I N D E X   R U T H E N I U M
G E O   P O R E   L I N T
H A N K A A R O N   S L A I N
T R E A T S     R E A S O N
      R O S E A T E   E N E
   B A R A C K O B A M A
B O A   G U A N A C O
E N C O D E   T E A B A G
T E T R A   S U P E R B O W L
   M E A L   E V E S   R N A
F O R T Y F O U R   H U M I D
E R I E   R U L E   I N A N E
D E A D   A L A S   T O N G S
```

Crossword Solutions

71

```
S N A R E   J E A N   A F A R
A E S O P   U C L A   S I M I
P H I L I P R O T H   S N I P
S I T E   E O N   B E I G E
      P A T R O B E R T S O N
S P I L L S   A B A S H
M E T A L   E U R O S   L A M
E A S Y   P R M E N   D I K E
E T A   W A R P S   L E N I N
    S T E N O   D E P E N D
P I E R R E R E N O I R
E M C E E   L I E   I V E S
D A R N   P A U L R E V E R E
A G E D   R I D E   G E N I E
L E T S   O D E S   O S I E R
```

72

```
R U N O F F   S A W S   C A B
S T A P L E   C R O P   O L E
T A M P E R P R O O F   M C I
    E S E   E A S E   S M O G
S O T   C O P P E R P L A T E
I N A H E A P   I E S T
R E P O   T E R R A C E
    S E M P E R P A R A T U S
      B U S S I N G   E N T S
    P A R R   C U D D L E S
P A P E R P U S H E R   I M S
E R A S   A N T E   Y A K
R I C   S U P E R P O W E R S
P A H   A S I A   S U N L I T
S H E   P E N D   I T S Y O U
```

73

```
A C T A S   A L P   S I E G E
S H A L T   B I C   C L A R A
T I K K I   C M L   I O T A S
O N E A R M   B A M   I S N T
    C L I M B   B A L L A D E
T R A I N S E T   R I O T E R
D A R N   G R A M S
S T E E R   T U B   P I P E S
    U C O N N   T R E E
W I E S E L   K E R O S E N E
E N D U S E R   R E N A L
T H E N   O A R   O L D A G E
T A N G O   N O R   O A T E N
E L I T E   B O O   A T E S T
D E C O R   Y T D   N E S T S
```

74

```
A P E   H I T C H   A D E P T
E R S   A C U R A   R E V U E
S I S I S E N O R   A B A T E
O M E N   J A P E   M I N T S
P A N A M A   F I T
    C M A J O R S C A L E
S L O P S   T U N E   A X O N
H O B O   F A L S E   R E N O
E V I L   E L I E   I D L E S
S E E Y O U L A T E R
    E N D   N E T T L E
P A S S E   O R C A   A R A B
E L I T E   S E A B R E E Z E
W I L E Y   H E L L O   E E R
S T O R E   A L L E N   D D T
```

75

```
A L T A R   T A P S   H G T S
D I O D E   A L O T   A R A L
Z Z T O P   L O L A   D O R A
      P U N C H A N D J U D Y
L E F T B E   A R L O   C Y S
I M A   L E E   E T C H
S O C K I T T O M E   F O C I
A T T I C   U A E   R O M A N
S E C T   H I T T H E S A C K
    H E L I   S E A   R T E
A W E   E G G S   E L I X I R
D E C K T H E H A L L S
M A K E   I N O N   I A M B S
E V E N   Q U O I   F I E R Y
N E R O   S S T S   E D G A R
```

The New York Times

Crossword Puzzles

The #1 Name in Crosswords

Available at your local bookstore or online at nytimes.com/nytstore

Coming Soon!

For the Love of Crosswords	978-1-250-02522-7
Sweet and Simple Crosswords	978-1-250-02525-8
Monday Crossword Puzzle Omnibus	978-1-250-02523-4
Tuesday Crossword Puzzle Omnibus	978-1-250-02526-5
Surrender to Sunday Crosswords	978-1-250-02524-1
Easiest Crosswords	978-1-250-02519-7
Will's Best	978-1-250-02531-9
Fast and Fresh Crosswords	978-1-250-02521-0
Easy Crossword Puzzle Volume 14	978-1-250-02520-3

Special Editions

Will Shortz Picks His Favorite Puzzles	978-0-312-64550-2
Crosswords for the Holidays	978-0-312-64544-1
Crossword Lovers Only: Easy Puzzles	978-0-312-54619-9
Crossword Lovers Only: Easy to Hard Puzzles	978-0-312-68139-5
Little Pink Book of Crosswords	978-0-312-65421-4
Little Black & White Book of Holiday Crosswords	978-0-312-65424-5
Little Black (and White) Book of Sunday Crosswords	978-0-312-59003-1
Will Shortz's Wittiest, Wackiest Crosswords	978-0-312-59034-5
Crosswords to Keep Your Brain Young	0-312-37658-8
Little Black (and White) Book of Crosswords	0-312-36105-X
Little Red and Green Book of Crosswords	0-312-37661-8
Little Flip Book of Crosswords	0-312-37043-1
How to Conquer the New York Times Crossword Puzzle	0-312-36554-3
Will Shortz's Favorite Crossword Puzzles	0-312-30613-X
Will Shortz's Favorite Sunday Crossword Puzzles	0-312-32488-X
Will Shortz's Greatest Hits	0-312-34242-X
Will Shortz Presents Crosswords for 365 Days	0-312-36121-1
Will Shortz's Funniest Crossword Puzzles Vol. 2	0-312-33960-7
Will Shortz's Funniest Crossword Puzzles	0-312-32489-8
Will Shortz's Xtreme Xwords	0-312-35203-4

Easy Crosswords

Easy Crossword Puzzles Vol. 13	978-1-250-00403-1
Easy Crossword Puzzles Vol. 12	978-0-312-68137-1
Volumes 2–11 also available	

Tough Crosswords

Tough Crossword Puzzles Vol. 13	0-312-34240-3
Tough Crossword Puzzles Vol. 12	0-312-32442-1
Volumes 9–11 also available	

Sunday Crosswords

Sweet Sunday Crosswords	978-1-250-01592-6
Sunday Crosswords Puzzles Vol. 38	978-1-250-01544-0
Sunday in the Surf Crosswords	978-1-250-00924-1
Simply Sundays	978-1-250-00390-4
Fireside Sunday Crosswords	978-0-312-64546-5
Snuggle Up Sunday Crosswords	978-0-312-59057-4
Stay in Bed Sunday Crosswords	978-0-312-68144-9
Relaxing Sunday Crosswords	978-0-312-65429-0
Finally Sunday Crosswords	978-0-312-64113-9
Crosswords for a Lazy Sunday	978-0-312-60820-0
Sunday's Best	0-312-37637-5
Sunday at Home Crosswords	0-312-37834-3

Omnibus

Easy to Not-So-Easy Crossword Puzzle Omnibus Vol. 6	978-1-250-00402-4
Day at the Beach Crossword Puzzle Omnibus	978-0-312-58843-4
Garden Party Crossword Puzzles	978-0-312-60824-8
Crossword Getaway	978-1-250-00928-9
Crosswords for Two	0-312-37830-0
Crosswords for a Relaxing Weekend	0-312-37829-7
Crosswords for a Lazy Afternoon	0-312-33108-8
Ultimate Crossword Omnibus	0-312-31622-4
Tough Crossword Puzzle Omnibus Vol. 1	0-312-32441-3
Crossword Challenge	0-312-33951-8
Crosswords for a Weekend Getaway	0-312-35198-4
Easy Crossword Puzzle Omnibus Vol. 8	978-1-250-00929-6
Crossword Puzzle Omnibus Vol. 16	0-312-36104-1
Sunday Crossword Omnibus Vol. 10	0-312-59006-7
Previous volumes also available	

Portable Size Format

Holiday Crosswords	978-1-250-01539-6
Crafty Crosswords	978-1-250-01541-9
Homestyle Crosswords	978-1-250-01543-3
Picnic Blanket Crosswords	978-1-250-00391-4
Scrumptiously Simple Crosswords	978-1-250-00393-5
Deliciously Doable Crosswords	978-1-250-00394-2
Delightfully Difficult Crosswords	978-1-250-00395-9
Huge Book of Easy Crosswords	978-1-250-00399-7
Springtime Solving Crosswords	978-1-250-00400-0
Cunning Crosswords	978-0-312-64543-4
Little Book of Lots of Crosswords	978-0-312-64548-9
Effortlessly Easy Crossword Puzzles	978-0-312-64545-8
Big, Bad Book of Crosswords	978-0-312-58841-0
Midsummer Night's Crosswords	978-0-312-58842-7
Early Morning Crosswords	978-0-312-58840-3
Pop Culture Crosswords	978-0-312-59059-8
Mad Hatter Crosswords	978-0-312-58847-2
Crosswords to Unwind Your Mind	978-0-312-68135-7
Keep Calm and Crossword On	978-0-312-68141-8
Light and Easy Crosswords	978-0-312-68142-5
Hot and Steamy Crosswords	978-0-312-68140-1
Big and Bold Crosswords	978-0-312-68134-0
Weekends with Will	978-0-312-65668-3
Every Day with Crosswords	978-0-312-65426-9
Clever Crosswords	978-0-312-65425-2
Everyday Easy Crosswords	978-0-312-64115-3
Puzzle Doctor Presents Crossword Fever	978-0-312-64110-8
Poolside Puzzles	978-0-312-64114-6
Sunny Crosswords	978-0-312-61446-0
Mild Crosswords	978-0-312-64117-7
Mellow Crosswords	978-0-312-64118-4
Mischievous Crosswords	978-0-312-64119-1
Wake Up with Crosswords	978-0-312-60819-4
Simply Soothing Crosswords	978-0-312-60823-1
Simply Satisfying Crosswords	978-0-312-60822-4
Simply Sneaky Crosswords	978-0-312-60821-7
ABCs of Crosswords	978-1-250-00922-7
Best of Monday Crosswords	978-1-250-00926-5
Best of Tuesday Crosswords	978-1-250-00927-2
Dreaming of Crosswords	978-1-250-00930-2
Mad About Crosswords	978-1-250-00923-4
All the Crosswords that Are Fit to Print	978-1-250-00925-8
Other volumes also available	

Made in United States
North Haven, CT
16 February 2022

16165648R00059